THE INNER COMPASS PROCESS

USING CHILDHOOD MEMORIES TO GUIDE YOUR CAREER CHANGE

DANIELLE ROESSLE

LCSW, GCDFI, CCSP

Copyright © 2021 by Inner Compass Press

All rights reserved. No part of this publication may be reproduced, distributed, or transmitted in any form or by any means, including photocopying, recording, or other electronic or mechanical methods, without the prior written permission of the publisher, except in the case of brief quotations embodied in critical reviews and certain other noncommercial uses permitted by copyright law. For permission requests, write to the author, addressed "Attention: Permissions" at info@innercompasscoach.com.

Cover and interior design by Victoria Wolf, wolfdesignandmarketing.com

Inner Compass Press
Bethesda, MD
innercompasspress.com

Ordering Information: innercompasscoach.com

ISBN: 978-1-7367176-0-8

To all my clients, thank you for sharing your stories with me and having the courage to make a fulfilling change. I dedicate this book to you. You have allowed me to hone the Inner Compass Process, put it out there for millions to read, and make a difference in the lives of others.

CONTENTS

Preface: My Inner Compass Story vii

Introduction: What is Your Inner Compass? 1

Part 1: Rediscovery

Your True North Guide: Helping you trust
your inner compass along this journey 17

Lesson 1: Play Your Way to Clarity Overview 21

Lesson 2: Your Freeing Mindset 39

Lesson 3: Your Binding Mindset 53

Lesson 4: Your Core Values 71

Lesson 5: Your Driving Talents 83

Lesson 6: Connect the Dots: Why You Do What You Do 99

Lesson 7: The Best Use of Your Time and Skills 105

Part 2: Career Exploration

Lesson 8: Jump in and Make a Change 131

Lesson 9: How to Do the Research 169

Lesson 10: Career Conversations 189

Part 3: Creating A Map Of Next Steps

Lesson 11: Narrowing Your Options 211

Lesson 12: Make a Post-It Timeline 223

Note from the Author 239

Needs Inventory 241

List of Feelings When Your Needs Are Satisfied 243

Positive Behaviors List 245

List of Feelings When Your Needs Are Not Satisfied 247

List of Negative Behaviors 249

List of Driving Talents 251

About the Author 253

Acknowledgments 255

References 257

PREFACE

MY INNER COMPASS STORY

MORE THAN TEN YEARS AGO, I worked as a high school social worker and was charged with teaching a college and careers class. When advising my students, I noticed they looked at jobs as a means of making money, not as something that could bring them a sense of purpose. I wanted them to have future jobs that truly fulfilled them.

The problem was, I didn't truly feel fulfilled in my work, either. I was burned out, tired of my long commute, and, as much as I loved working with students, I just felt like something was missing.

I decided to do what I had wanted for my students – to find my life's purpose, or career calling.

Since I had worked as a clinical social worker, I did what I knew best. I enrolled in career development, psychology, and life coaching courses to find my life's purpose.

I didn't know it at the time, but all of these courses built a foundation for a career coaching business that I would start in 2013.

When I had just started my career coaching business, I participated in a course facilitated by Bobby Woods, founder of Spirit Aura, on finding your life's purpose. The workshop was held at a yoga studio in Denver, Colorado. All the participants sat on pillows on the floor, and the walls were adorned with multicolored tapestries.

During Bobby's workshop, he had us revisit our most difficult childhood memories. I volunteered to be the guinea pig and, in front of fifteen people, recalled an incident when three girls had bullied me in fourth grade by taping a thumbtack on my chair. I remembered thinking, *No one likes me, and no one ever will.* When I told the teacher, she scolded the girls, but there was ultimately no recourse. I realized how much I desperately wanted connection and how alone I felt at that time in my life. I also felt unsafe in my surroundings and thought that grownups wouldn't protect me.

Bobby asked me what my life purpose was, based on what happened to me. I looked at him, confused, and I told him I didn't know. He responded, "Danielle, you are meant to be a connector. You wanted a connection with those girls and the world around you. You are meant to help others find that connection." I let his words sink in.

I realized that I had always been a connector, whether it had been organizing events for my youth group, playing matchmaker in my twenties, or as a social worker supporting my students. I had always found a way to be a connector, regardless of whether I was being paid for it or not. I had been focused on finding a dream job to live out my life's purpose. It turns out that I was *already* living out my life's purpose by using my innate talents as a connector.

In this book, you will see that you are already living out your life's purpose by using your innate, motivating talents. I call these natural, motivating gifts "Driving Talents." You've been using them for your entire life, because they are a part of who you are.

I became fascinated with the connection between our most painful memories and our innate gifts and began asking my clients to recall some of the obstacles they had to overcome in childhood. I labeled the feelings, thoughts, and behaviors associated with negative memories as their "Binding Mindset." I found that their Binding Mindset from childhood was usually holding them back from career fulfillment today. And, more often than not, their painful memories revealed their Driving Talents.

In 2014, I met Nora A'Bel of Revenue Tribe. Nora was working with entrepreneurs to help them gain clarity on integrating purpose into their work. While Bobby had helped me see the silver lining of my negative memories, Nora's work unpacked the impact of positive memories on forming beliefs. It provided the framework of what I now call the "Freeing Mindset," or the feelings, thoughts, and behaviors that you associate with being fulfilled.

Nora had me recall a memory of hiking in Dickerson, Maryland, with my family when I was around age eight. We had climbed to the top of Sugarloaf Mountain, and I remember thinking, *My family really loves me*. I felt warm and open-hearted, smiled a lot, and was very talkative.

When working with Nora, I realized that I wanted to think, feel, and behave the same way in my career as I did in my happy childhood memories. I learned that my positive memories revealed my Driving Talents as well, because they showed how much I need connection in my life. To this day, I create experiences that facilitate positive connection, whether that be workshops for my clients or events for my friends.

The missing piece that finally wove my work together was when I read *Nonviolent Communication: A Language of Life*, by Dr. Marshall Rosenberg in 2016. Dr. Rosenberg explains that communication breakdowns happen because people don't know how to express their needs. Humans' reactions and behaviors are motivated by their needs.

Upon reading this, I realized that my deep needs come from my childhood experiences. When I reflected on my memories, I could see the needs that motivated me in those moments. My deep needs for connection, belonging, and creativity are so intrinsic to who I am that meeting them is essential for career happiness. I call these deep needs "core values."

Your Driving Talents, core values, and Freeing and Binding Mindsets are the unchanging pieces that will always guide you toward career fulfillment. I call this your True North.

While my deep needs never change, my other needs adjust as my life evolves. When I started my business as a career coach seven years ago, I had a social work degree and experience in career counseling, but working for someone else couldn't fulfill my needs for financial independence and security. I used my Driving Talents for connection and creativity to build my business to meet those needs.

THE INNER COMPASS PROCESS

Now that I've worked for myself for seven years, moved across the country, and married my partner, my needs have shifted. Now I need more joy and lightness in my life. As a result, I took a part-time job at a high school as a college counselor. I am still using my Driving Talents of connection and creativity but in a new and refreshing way.

I created the Inner Compass Process to help you connect with your inner compass and uncover your life's purpose. Your career will shift and evolve as you do.

Your childhood memories, both happy and unhappy, will provide immense insight into what comes naturally to you in your career—what fulfills and motivates you, and the impact you want to make through your career. I'll be sharing more pieces of my own story and some client stories throughout this book to illustrate this process.

This book will guide you to connect the dots between your past, present, and future—to tell the important stories that provide insight into who you are today and who you want to be tomorrow. You will come away with a well-calibrated inner compass that directs you to career options that serve your deepest needs, make use of your Driving Talents, and keep you feeling your best.

My wish for you is that you embrace all parts of yourself, because once you do, you are home.

With love,
Danielle

INTRODUCTION

WHAT IS YOUR INNER COMPASS?

YOUR INNER COMPASS IS your deepest inner voice. It's also known in psychology as your psyche, the connection of your mind, heart, and intuition, or your higher self. It's the voice that shares your true likes, dislikes, and needs. You developed it in childhood and learned to ignore it as everyone else put their judgments, opinions, and expectations on you.

In this book, you will reconnect with your inner compass by revisiting various experiences throughout your childhood and career and uncovering the patterns that allow you to thrive and those that hold you back. You'll identify your Freeing Mindset (the feelings, thoughts, and behaviors that you associate with being fulfilled) and your Binding Mindset (the feelings, thoughts, and behaviors that you associate with being unfulfilled). You will better understand your core values and your Driving Talents. Then, using your newfound understanding as your True North, you will make changes in your work to experience greater fulfillment.

WHAT IS THE PSYCHOLOGY BEHIND THIS BOOK?

This book is based on inner-child work, which is used in psychology to heal trauma and disrupt dysfunctional behavioral patterns. When I started integrating inner-child work into career counseling, my clients had profound insights as to how their childhoods affected their careers. They shifted from being stuck to having more clarity.

So, you might wonder, "What is my inner child, and why would I want to connect with it?"

Your inner child is who you were as a kid that has gotten lost along the way. While reading this book, you will revisit your inner child and share stories of the events in your life that were formative and shaped your identity today.

By visiting and getting to know your inner child, you will better understand what has been influencing your career decisions. You will realize what motivates you, what holds you back, and what makes you want to get out of bed every day and go to work. The more you converse with, and get to know, your inner child, the more you will free yourself.

Inner-child work originated with Carl Jung, a Swiss psychiatrist and psychoanalyst who was a contemporary of Sigmund Freud in the early 1900s. Jung developed the "child archetypes," the idea that we have distinct personalities within us, both conscious and unconscious.

Jung named the multiple child archetypes and used them to explain why we do what we do. Some examples of Jung's archetypes are the Ruler, Creator/Artist, Sage, Innocent, Explorer, Rebel, Hero, Wizard, Jester, Everyman, Lover, and Caregiver.

Many more archetypes have been researched and developed by various psychologists since Jung's original ideas. In the 1970s, art therapist Lucia Capacchione explored Jung's archetypes and introduced the concept of "reparenting" the inner child or giving yourself the self-love and support that you may not have received as a child.

The inner-child concept informs other therapeutic models, such as Internal Family Systems (IFS) developed by Richard C. Schwartz in the 1990s, which explores how the different subpersonalities in your mind interact with one another. Schwartz's concept is to rediscover your core Self, or the grounded, compassionate, and confident part of you.

This book is an opportunity for you to reconnect with your inner child. Just as I've done with many clients, I will ask you targeted questions to help you better understand what you want and need, similar to Lucia Capacchione's process of reparenting. This book is also an invitation to make up for what has been lost in your career so you can live as your true self, like Richard C. Schwartz's concept of rediscovering your core self. It is never too late to make a pivot to feel more fulfilled!

THIS BOOK IS FOR YOU IF…

- You've been feeling stuck and unsure where to go next regarding your career.
- You've been in your career for at least two years and know you aren't fulfilled.
- You want to be intentional about your career next steps and have a clear direction.
- You are open to digging deep and going back to your childhood to reconnect with the true you.
- You want to identify what's working and not working in your career.
- You want to feel more confident in your talents and skills.
- You want to feel motivated and fulfilled by your work.
- You want to be paid for your natural abilities and live out your life's purpose.
- You want to create a plan for making a change, but you're unsure how to do it.
- If any of those statements ring true for you, the Inner Compass Process is for you.

THIS BOOK IS NOT FOR YOU IF…

- You do not want to dig deep and go back to your childhood.
- You want someone to give you the answers.
- You're in a rush to make money.
- You want to learn how to write a cover letter and résumé.

WHAT THIS BOOK WILL DO FOR YOU

This book will take you through a step-by-step process to rediscover who you really are, help you identify what is working and not working in your career, and clarify your career direction.

You will:
- Go back to childhood to clarify what you want and need in a career. You will have a lot of "aha" moments.
- Clarify your Freeing Mindset, or your definition of fulfillment.
- Identify your four core values from childhood and recognize the signs that a potential employer shares your values.
- Uncover your Driving Talent(s), or the one or two natural gifts that drive you to get out of bed every morning; they are your purpose and what you want to be paid for in your career.
- Narrow down your search to one or two fulfilling career options.
- Envision your ideal workday and the qualities that allow you to thrive in your career.
- Become a detective, researcher, and master networker and find strategies to test the waters so that you feel confident in your new career direction.
- Create an actionable plan for achieving your career goals.

ABOUT THE INNER COMPASS PROCESS

The Inner Compass Process is made up of three parts: Rediscovery, Career Exploration, and Creating a Map of Next Steps.

Part 1: Rediscovery

First, you will share stories from your childhood and your career to help you identify the qualities that you need to thrive at work. You'll discover your core values and your Driving Talents.

Part 2: Career Exploration

Next, you'll determine what changes you want to make, whether that's moving to a new job, career, employer, industry, or starting a business. You will learn various strategies to ensure your career change is aligned with your needs.

Part 3: Creating a Map of Next Steps

Lastly, you will map out your timeline. Your timeline will include realistic goals, strategies to accomplish your goals, and tactics to overcome obstacles that might get in your way.

As you work through this book, you will complete your True North Guide.

Your True North Guide is a document where you will gather the insights you have about what you need to thrive at work. Each lesson in the first section will provide an essential piece of your True North Guide. In the end, your guide will be a document you can use to make sure you're headed in a direction that will be more fulfilling and meaningful.

Throughout this process, I will share parts of my story to guide you through the exercises. By reading parts of my story, you will see that you are not alone. My story is there to help you better understand yourself and what you need from your career.

HOW TO COMPLETE THIS BOOK

This book should take about six weeks to complete. Most readers will complete two lessons a week. Each lesson builds on the previous one; however, if you're finding yourself struggling with a concept, keep going. Most readers find more clarity as they continue through this book.

In the first three lessons, you will go back to memories of your childhood and career and answer questions about those memories. In the beginning, you may find your answers are broad. However, as you continue, patterns will emerge. You will be able to hone your responses as your self-knowledge grows.

I recommend that you dedicate three to four hours a week to focus on Lessons 1-10.

As you move to Lessons 10–12, devote five to six hours a week to research careers and schedule time for career conversations.

HOW TO USE THE ICONS

Throughout the lessons, you will find three types of icons:

The journaling icon is an invitation to take some time to write down your response to one of the questions. There will be a lot of reflective questions throughout this book to help you gain career clarity.

The compass icon directs you to take your response and add it to your True North Guide on pages 18-20.

The email icon indicates to copy and paste the text into an email. You will be reaching out to others and asking for their feedback to help you home in on your career direction.

THE GUIDING CONCEPTS

Understanding several guiding concepts will help you move through this book with ease, be realistic about your career change, and set you up for success.

Let Your Needs Guide You

Our society teaches us to ignore our needs, and, unfortunately, the act of taking care of our needs gets a bad rap. We are told not to be needy and to put others' needs above our own.

However, needs are an intrinsic part of being human. We come out of the womb with physical and emotional needs, such as food, shelter, sleep, warmth, love, and connection, and we depend on others to fulfill them. As we grow older, we learn how to meet our basic needs, while often ignoring our emotional needs.

Meeting your needs is a key component of being happy in your career. In this book you will learn to identify your needs to find ways to shift your career and experience more fulfillment.

Take the example of a real estate agent named Ronda. Ronda was a fifty-two-year-old single mom who had been a real estate agent for twenty-three years and had built a lucrative business that could provide for her family. She had put her daughter through college and cared for her aging mother until she passed away.

Ronda pursued career coaching with me because she was completely burned out and was unsure of where she wanted to go next. She shared that she lacked patience for the home buying-and-selling process and felt little empathy for her clients. She realized that she had put everyone else's needs in front of hers for years. While her career met her basic need for financial stability, it did not meet her emotional need for meaning.

Ronda's career allowed her to afford the life she wanted to give to her daughter and to care for her mother. But now that Ronda had few obligations, she wanted more for herself. She wanted her last working years to make an impact and be meaningful, but she didn't know what career would do it.

Ronda had a difficult childhood. Her father left her family at an early age, and her mother was often busy. Ronda spent a lot of time at church, where she felt connected to the greater community. Ronda loved everything about her church, from the community dinners to singing in the choir to volunteering.

Ronda's church met her core needs for community and contribution. I asked if those needs were being met through her real estate career. She said that her real estate career met her need for community at one time, but not anymore, and she acknowledged that her career had never met her need for contribution. She realized that she needed to shift her career to honor her core emotional needs.

Ronda began volunteering for a local nonprofit in fundraising and eventually transitioned into a donor relations position after a year. While the job was not as lucrative as her real estate career, it honored her emotional needs.

For the Inner Compass Process to work, you must give yourself permission to explore your needs and tell yourself they matter. This book will examine your needs in depth—the consistent needs that you've had your entire life and that form your core values. We'll also explore the needs that shift over time, depending on your stage of life.

Lead with your Driving Talents

The career coaching world often says that your job should pay you for your passions. It's not bad advice; it's just confusing.

Here's why the advice to follow your passions is confusing. 1) You might have multiple passions and they may change over time; 2) Not all your passions can be turned into a legitimate career; 3) You might not like the reality of the career that follows your passions.

Instead of following your passions, I propose that you identify your Driving Talents and pursue work in which you're paid for them. Your Driving Talents are your innate abilities that give you so much satisfaction and fulfillment, you want to go to work so you can use them.

Your "life purpose" is to manifest your Driving Talents in a way that feels authentic to you and to let them shine. How they shine will depend on the season of your life and your needs.

For example, your Driving Talent might be teaching. You can teach in many capacities — in a traditional classroom setting with students, as a corporate trainer, self-employed tutor, or in another position. The position you choose will depend on what your inner compass is telling you.

We'll be looking at how you liked to play as a child, your happiest childhood memories, and your negative memories of childhood to clarify your Driving Talents.

Take the example of John. John became passionate about environmental injustice when he was an undergraduate at college. He ran the environmental club and engaged the student body to make changes on campus.

Since John thought he should follow his passions, he took the LSAT and went to law school to become an environmental lawyer.

Twelve years later, he was completely burned out. He hated the politics of environmental nonprofits, think tanks, and political organizations. He shared that his job's reality was very different from the idea he had of it in college.

When working through the Inner Compass Process, John explored how he liked problem solving and what came naturally to him (his Driving Talents). As he reflected on his childhood and career stories, he realized that he enjoyed organizing people and managing projects. His ability to organize gave him a sense of competence and achievement.

While John did use his Driving Talents minimally in his law career, he was paid primarily to research and litigate. When John changed his focus to what came naturally to him, moving to a career in people and project management was an obvious and fulfilling option. He transitioned out of environmental law and began working for a tech employer with a strong sustainability initiative.

John shared how surprised he was to feel so much more fulfilled in his job at a tech employer. He thought that working as an environmental lawyer would make him fulfilled, because environmental law has a mission he shares. However, using his Driving Talents in his work made him feel much more fulfilled, because he was doing work that was more aligned with his natural problem-solving abilities.

After you've identified your Driving Talents in the next few lessons, you will have a much clearer idea of what will make you feel fulfilled. You may be surprised at the options that present themselves once you have a better understanding of your innate, motivating talents.

Stop Looking for Your "Career Calling" or "Dream Job"

We often use heavy language to describe our careers. How many times have you heard "find your dream job," or "find your career calling"? This language suggests heavy expectations of how things should be and often leads to disappointment.

These concepts don't consider that things continuously change, both in our lives and the world around us. Our needs will change as we shift into different seasons of our lives, so our concept of career should evolve as we do.

The idea of a dream job implies that we have arrived and that one job will fulfill all our needs for the rest of our lives.

Let's look at Jennifer's experience. When she was twenty-eight years old, Jennifer worked as an event planner at one of the famous hotel chains. She could not believe she had landed her dream job just after graduating from college. At her event planning job, she used her Driving Talent of inclusion by including others and making them feel welcome.

Then the COVID-19 pandemic hit the United States, and Jennifer's job was eliminated. She interviewed for several remote conference planner jobs but felt the online coordination would not give her the same sense of satisfaction because her roles and responsibilities had changed.

When Jennifer opened up to the possibility that other jobs could meet her needs and provide her the same sense of fulfillment, she was excited to explore her options. Jennifer found that human resources (HR) offered many opportunities to meet her needs for connection, competency, and engagement. HR also allowed her to use her Driving Talent of inclusion.

Jennifer said that while she loved her former job as an event planner, she and her husband were considering having children and that the long hours of working evenings and weekends would not be suitable for a family. She was excited that human resources could meet her newfound need for flexibility.

The job market will continue to change through world events, technology, and globalization. Some careers will evolve with these changes, while others will cease to exist.

If you open up to the possibility that many job options can bring you fulfillment and tap your Driving Talents, then it's a matter of identifying what you need, what you're good at, and understanding the options available to you.

Be Open to Different Types of Career Changes

My clients often believe that to fulfill their needs, they must change careers. As you read through this book, you might find that a big change is unnecessary. You might only need to change your job, employer, or industry. You may even find that you can change your mindset and be happy in your current job.

If making a significant change feels stressful to you, perhaps make incremental changes instead, such as taking on different roles and responsibilities, changing positions within your employer, or finding a similar job at another employer.

For example, Brianne, an operations manager at a recreation center, felt dissatisfied in her role because she believed her work deserved a higher salary. Brianne thought she would have to change careers to achieve a higher salary, but after completing the Inner Compass Process, she realized that she could have her financial needs met as an operations manager elsewhere. She ended up switching into the private sector and received a ten percent pay increase.

KEY TERMS

At the end of each lesson, I will leave you with a few questions to think about when it comes to your work situation. You may decide to change your job, employer, career, industry, or start a business.

I find that many clients think they want to make a huge change, but after doing the Inner Compass Process, they find that smaller changes might serve them better, such as changing aspects of their job or employer. On the other hand, some clients need to make significant changes, such as changing their careers or industries.

Take a look at the terms below, so you can have a framework of what you'll be evaluating as you work through this book.

Your job

The term "job" refers to the roles and responsibilities you do every day. It's how you spend your time.

Your career

Your "career" is the various jobs that you can have with your current skill set, education, and training. It's also the jobs that are related to your current job that you can transition into with additional education and training.

For example, a software engineer's career could include titles such as senior software engineer, senior software engineer developer, lead software engineer, principal software engineer, and VP of software development.

Your employer

Your "employer" is the place in which you work. It is the company, organization, agency, institution, or business in which you are employed.

Your industry

Your "industry" is the type of goods and services your employer produces. Some examples of industries are food services, agriculture, entertainment, recreation, construction, data processing, education, healthcare, finance, hospitals, hospitality, manufacturing, oil and gas, transportation, and utilities.

BEFORE WE GET STARTED, ASK FOR FEEDBACK FROM FRIENDS, FAMILY, AND COWORKERS.

To identify your Driving Talents, in Lesson 5 of this book, you will survey friends, family, and coworkers about what they think of your strengths and skills. Copy and paste the email below and then send it to at least four friends, family members, and coworkers. One to two people you send it to should be friends or family, and the others should be coworkers or people you know in a professional capacity.

Please only send this survey to people who will give you good feedback and don't have a stake in your career choices. For example, don't send it to a spouse who would be anxious about you making a change or a parent who just wants you to stay put because it's "safer."

Even though you won't use the survey responses until Lesson 5, I want you to ask them for feedback now, so you'll have their responses when we need them later.

In Lesson 5, I will walk you through the process I use with clients to help you unpack and understand the responses you receive.

Dear x,

I am participating in a professional development course to evaluate my talents and abilities to better stand out in my career.

Would you take a few minutes to provide some feedback through this survey? Any insights would be much appreciated! Please submit your responses no later than (date). Thank you for your time.

1. What is my top gift or talent? Am I gifted at advising, analyzing, building, cheerleading, coaching, connecting, contributing, creating, designing, implementing, intuiting, inventing, leading, listening, logistics, mediating, networking, peacemaking, strategizing, thinking, or something else?
2. What adjectives would you use to describe me to someone else? (This can include character traits.)
3. Can you share some examples of when I used my top gifts or talents?
4. When have you noticed me most fulfilled in my work? What was I doing?
5. When have you noticed me most discontent in my work? What were the circumstances?
6. What do you think I should do for a living, and how do you see my career evolving? Why?

*Note—If you have been out of the workforce for some time, you can modify questions 4 and 5 by removing or replacing "work" with something else like "volunteering."

PART 1

REDISCOVERY

YOUR TRUE NORTH GUIDE

HELPING YOU TRUST YOUR INNER COMPASS ALONG THIS JOURNEY.

AS WE JOURNEY THROUGH THIS BOOK, you'll be completing your True North Guide. This guide helps you see what works for you in your career and what to avoid. It also allows you to envision your ideal day at work.

Keep your True North Guide close as you continue this journey. Use it to point you toward jobs that are a good fit for you and away from those that will take you off track.

Remember, your True North Guide is an evolving document. You may shift and change parts of it as you go through this process. That's perfectly fine! It's all part of the journey of recalibrating your inner compass.

Since job titles and culture can differ from one employer to the next, your True North Guide will provide a framework for the qualities you are seeking.

YOUR TRUE NORTH GUIDE

Your Driving Talents (Natural Problem-Solving Abilities) (page 89):

Your Freeing Mindset™ (Fulfilling Behavioral Patterns) (page 48):

I feel:

I think:

I behave:

Your Binding Mindset™ (Unfulfilling Behavioral Patterns) (page 63):

I feel:

I think:

I behave:

Your Core Values (Core Beliefs) (page 76):

Your Needs Now (page 78):

The impact or contribution you want to make through your work (page 81):

Your Job Likes (Former Roles and Responsibilities You Liked) (page 109):

Your Job Dislikes (Former Roles and Responsibilities You Should Avoid) (page 109):

Your On-Fire Skills (The Best Use of Your Time and Talents) (page 123): %

Your Heating Up Skills (Skills You Want to Build) (page 125): %

Your Burnout Skills (What You Need to Let Go of or Minimize) (page 127):

Roles and Responsibilities You've Never Had That You Want:

Your Ideal Salary (Immediate and Future Salary Goals):

Job Titles, Businesses, or Educational Options You Want to Target:

Your Next Move (The Change You Want to Commit to) (page 222):

LESSON 1

PLAY YOUR WAY
TO CLARITY OVERVIEW

YOU MAY BE WONDERING WHY a book about work starts with a lesson about play. This book will take you on a journey to deepen your self-understanding as you explore what fulfills your needs and excites you. What better place to start clarifying your career direction than with play, or your preferred way of enjoying yourself in your free time?

Play helps you develop a healthy mind, body, and relationships, which are essential for your ability to thrive in society. Research also shows that play helps you increase your creativity, agility, communication skills, social skills, and emotional intelligence, forming a foundation for you to excel in your work.[1]

When you explore the ways you liked to play in childhood and how you like to spend your time in adulthood, you open a window for understanding what fills you with joy and vitality. You also gain insight into facets of your personality that can help you shine in your career.

> How you liked to play as a child might shed light on interests you want to draw upon in your career.

Children explore the world with curiosity and unapologetic expression, entirely in the moment. Children continue to do activities that they enjoy, that interest them, and that come naturally to them. They discontinue activities when they feel bored, uninterested, or frustrated. Play provides insights into what you naturally enjoy. Your childhood preferences likely still show up to this day.

If you enjoyed arts and crafts as a child, your career might need elements of creativity or design. If you loved movement and sports, your job might need some form of physicality. If you delighted in building objects, puzzles, or tinkering on computers, your job might need similar ways of problem solving. These are a few examples of how your childhood interests might have a direct connection to your career interests.

For example, Brad, age twenty-four, who self-identifies as queer, fell into customer service at age twenty because a friend referred him to the job. Brad completed one year of college but felt school wasn't for him because he wasn't a traditional learner. While he enjoyed the social aspects of his job, he couldn't see himself becoming a supervisor. He also shared that he hated sitting for long periods to complete the administrative aspects of his job, and he felt fidgety.

Brad loved styling dolls' hair when he was around six to eight years old, and then dyeing and styling his friends' hair in middle and high school. Even as an adult, Brad watches hair videos on Facebook, Instagram, TikTok, and YouTube.

Brad had considered becoming a hairstylist but felt compelled to get a degree because he wasn't sure he could make enough money. During the Career Conversations section of the Inner Compass Process (Lesson 10), Brad spoke to multiple successful hairstylists and discovered that he could make a lucrative career out of his interests. He enrolled in cosmetology school and eventually niched in curly hair.

When I spoke to Brad several years after completing career coaching together, he shared that going to work felt like he was being paid to play all day. Choosing to become a hairstylist was an act of embracing his identity. In Brad's case, his interests manifested directly in his career choice.

> How you liked to play as a child might provide insights into your personality or the personal qualities that you want to come out in your career.

Children develop social-emotional skills through playing with others. Through sports, games, and imaginative play, they learn communication, teamwork, and empathy.[1] When you observe a child playing with others, you will notice how they like to engage socially. Some children are more introverted and derive their energy from being by themselves, while others get energized from being with others. They may prefer one-on-one, small-group, or large-group play.

When you explore the way you liked to play as a child, you will better understand how you want to work and engage with others.

You might also recognize the different traits that form your personality. As a child, you might have been adventurous, chatty, compassionate, curious, deep-thinking, easygoing, inventive, practical, or witty. Some of these traits carry over into adulthood and need to be expressed in one's career.

Take the example of Maria, age forty-four, who self-identifies as Latinx. Maria worked in office administration for three years after spending eight years staying at home raising her children. She had taken an administrative position because she thought that was the only thing she was qualified to do after taking time away from the workforce. Maria was bored and under-challenged as an administrator and felt she wasn't using her natural abilities.

When we explored the ways Maria like to play as a child, we learned that she was always singing, dancing, and performing. She directed and acted in plays for her family, and she participated in theater in high school. She even shared that she was a nationally recognized Latina ballroom dancer in high school.

Maria moved away from performance in college because she was told to pursue something practical, such as a business degree. She met her husband in college and eventually left the workforce to raise her children. Even as an adult, Maria loved being in the spotlight with her friends and family. The qualities she wanted to embody in her career were her ability to perform, speak in front of others, and effectively communicate.

Maria ended up switching careers into educational sales, where she could persuade others, make sales presentations, and interact with the world in a way that felt authentic. In the case of Maria, her newly found sales career reflected her personality.

How you liked to play as a child can illuminate how you might bring more fulfillment to your free time, or that you might need more free time.

As you transition into adulthood, your play evolves with your psychological and physical development, yet remains just as important. Play in adulthood can come in the form of hobbies, activities, sports, and recreation. When you play, you release stress. Depending on how you like to play, it may encourage creativity, give you a chance to move your body, or provide opportunities for social connection.

Sadly, many adults don't get enough playtime. Many careers are demanding, with long hours and increased roles and responsibilities, leaving you with little time or energy to fill your cup. Lack of play creates disconnection from yourself and leaves needs unmet.

I've asked many clients what they do after a long day of work. Often, they share that they drink wine or beer with dinner, watch TV, and go to sleep. Food, drink, and television meet the basic needs for rest and sustenance. However, needs such as creativity, movement, challenge, and self-expression must be met by play.

My clients often find they need to change the way they spend their free time or that they need *more* free time. We must find more ways to bring fulfillment and/or meaning into all aspects of our lives.

One of the first homework assignments I give my clients is to incorporate more play into their lives. This assignment brings tremendous insight into what interests them, which might directly correlate to their career. It also starts helping them feel better because some of their needs are being addressed. My wish is for you to feel that way, too.

During this lesson, you will reflect on how play can shed light on your interests, your personality, and Driving Talents; and how you might find more fulfillment both personally and professionally.

A BLAST TO YOUR PAST

Take some time to reflect on how you liked to play as a child, ages four through twelve, or kindergarten through sixth grade. Think about how your play progressed from kindergarten through high school.

When exploring my play between the ages of four and twelve, I remembered that I loved riding my bike outside, hiking, and going on adventures. I also liked completing art projects and attending art classes. As I transitioned into middle and high school, I enjoyed running cross-country, hiking, and participating in youth group. I had one or two close friends, so I preferred one-on-one engagement. I was a curious, creative, active, and friendly little kid.

Michael, a twenty-six-year-old sales representative, loved building LEGOs, Erector sets, and forts in his backyard when he was a kid. He preferred a lot of alone time. As he transitioned into high school, his favorite class was woodworking, and he would spend hours with his instructor learning how to make furniture after school. Michael described himself as inventive, creative, independent, and adaptable as a child.

Josh, a thirty-eight-year-old mortgage broker, enjoyed playing sports as a kid—flag football, soccer, basketball, hockey, and lacrosse. He also volunteered with his family and friends at church. As he transitioned into middle and high school, he prided himself on becoming the captain of his football team and participating in various leadership roles. He had many friends and loved socializing in big groups. Josh described himself as social, happy-go-lucky, and athletic.

Now it's your turn. How did you like to play as a child? What were your interests? What was your personality? Did you enjoy creative play, such as journaling, writing, singing, crafting, dancing, making art, or performing? Did you like moving your body by participating in sports and movement? Did you lose track of time in logic-based activities, such as puzzles, video games, and computers? Did you act out a particular role, such as teacher, leader, queen, king, princess, prince, business owner, parent, construction worker, or superhero when you participated in imaginative play? Did you like being alone, with your friends, or a mix of both?

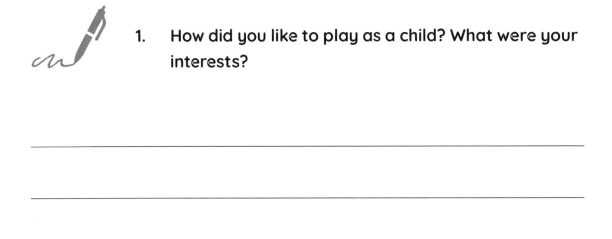

1. **How did you like to play as a child? What were your interests?**

___

___

___

2. **What was your personality like as a child, specifically when you would play and lose track of time?**

- Were you introverted or extroverted? Did you derive energy by being by yourself, being with others, or a mix of both?
- Did you prefer one-on-one, small-group, or large-group play?

- What personality traits or adjectives would you use to describe yourself as a kid when you would lose track of time playing? Were you adventurous, deep-thinking, easygoing, chatty, curious, compassionate, inventive, practical, or witty?
- Were there specific roles that you liked to play, such as leader, teacher, supporter, explorer, performer, etc.?

_____

_____

_____

NOW

How do you like to spend your free time as an adult? What are your interests? What do you do in your spare time?

Even as an adult, I love movement and enjoy walking, hiking, and other outdoor activities. I stay involved with my spiritual community and meditate regularly. I have a strong interest in personal growth, spirituality, and wellness. I still prefer one-on-one time with my friends. I would describe my personality as spiritual, reflective, friendly, curious, adventurous, and resourceful.

Michael, the twenty-six-year-old sales representative, continues to build furniture in his free time. He also loves to go fishing, hiking, and camping. He describes himself as a homebody yet independent, creative, and inventive.

Josh, the thirty-eight-year-old mortgage broker, shared that he enjoys working out at the gym and staying fit as an adult. While he isn't playing team sports anymore, watching sports with his friends brings fun and excitement and still gives him a sense of being on a team. Josh described himself as a social and easygoing adult.

Now it's your turn. Do you like to be creative and play music, journal, craft, cook, or act in your local theater troupe? Are you athletic, preferring to be outdoors, exercising, or going to the gym? Do you decompress through puzzles, video games, or playing on your computer? Maybe you like to travel or go on excursions to historical sights? Do you like being alone, with your friends and loved ones, or a mix of both?

3. **How do you like to play as an adult? What are your interests?**

_____

_____

_____

4. **What is your personality like now?**

- Are you introverted or extroverted? Do you derive energy by being by yourself, being with others, or a mix of both?
- Do you prefer one-on-one meetings, small groups, or large groups?
- What personality traits or adjectives would you use to describe yourself now when you are enjoying your time? Are you adventurous, deep-thinking, easy-going, chatty, curious, compassionate, inventive, practical, or witty?
- Are there specific roles you prefer to see yourself in, such as a leader, teacher, supporter, explorer, performer, etc.?

CONNECTING THE DOTS

Most people's play from childhood and adulthood have similarities. You might share similar interests with your younger self, some qualities of your personality may remain the same, or maybe there's a role you've embodied all your life.

When I compared my childhood play to my adult play, I noticed that I still love being outdoors, riding my bike, and going on adventures. While my spirituality has evolved, it's always been an important aspect of my life, shifting from childhood youth group to involvement with a spiritual community now. My personality remains similar in that I'm reflective, friendly, curious, adventurous, and resourceful. I still prefer one-on-one or small-group engagement.

Michael, the twenty-six-year-old sales representative, realized that he has been building things his whole life in some form or another. He had always been more introverted and preferred quiet time for inventing and building. He shared that his personality has always been more independent, creative, and inventive.

Josh, the thirty-eight-year-old mortgage broker, noticed that his love for sports never changed from childhood to adulthood and that the team aspect of it remained important to him. He had always been outgoing and preferred being in groups. He shared that he missed volunteering and engaging in community service. He recognized that he has always been easygoing and finds himself a natural leader both at work and among his friends.

5. **What do play in childhood and adulthood have in common?**

_____

_____

_____

When you look at how you have liked to play throughout your life, it fulfills some essential needs. My play meets my needs for connection, engagement, novelty, creativity, and community. Michael's play meets his needs for movement, creativity, and craftsmanship. Josh's play satisfies his needs for camaraderie, respect, purpose, contribution, and physical well-being.

When you explore your play from childhood and adulthood, what needs are being addressed? Connection, belonging, communication, closeness, community, companionship, respect, support, physical well-being, air, movement, freedom, independence, discovery, self-expression, stimulation, or something else?

6. When you explore play from childhood and adulthood, what needs are being addressed by the playing?

For a complete list of needs, please reference page 241.

___

___

___

YOUR DRIVING TALENTS

> Your Driving Talents are your innate abilities that give you so much satisfaction and fulfillment, you want to go to work so you can use them.

Your Driving Talents have been part of you for your entire life, and you can find them in the memories of play that you just explored. They may be hard to see because you probably take them for granted, and it might never have occurred to you that you should be paid to use them.

A fulfilling career will capitalize on your Driving Talents. The trick is identifying and pivoting your career to use them fully.

While you may be good at a lot of things, **your Driving Talents are the one or two abilities you have that seem effortless**. Solving problems at work feels easy and natural when you use your Driving Talents. They aren't just talents but lifelong traits that can be traced back to your childhood stories.

Your personality orients you to be good at your Driving Talents. Let's say your Driving Talent is thinking. Your personality might be analytical, observant, and intuitive. If your Driving Talent is mediating, your personality might be calm, observant, reflective and easygoing.

As a kid, I liked completing art projects and attending art classes. As I transitioned to middle and high school, I enjoyed creating programs for my youth group. One of my Driving Talents is my ability to create, whether I'm creating courses for clients or writing a book such as this one. When I create, the parts of my personality that come out are my curiosity, intuitive nature, and ability to collaborate with others.

Michael, the twenty-six-year-old sales representative, had a Driving Talent for building. He loved playing with Legos and Erector sets as a kid and enjoys building furniture as an adult. Building things motivates him deeply and gives him a deep sense of fulfillment. Michael's personality that comes out when he builds things are his independence, creativity, and ingenuity.

Josh, a thirty-eight-year-old mortgage broker, enjoyed volunteering and leading others in sports as a kid. He also enjoys mentoring mortgage brokers at his job. Josh's Driving Talent is his ability to lead. His easygoing, outgoing, and playful nature emerges when using his Driving Talents.

Now it's your turn. What Driving Talent (or talents) emerge in the way you like to play? Are you talented at advising, analyzing, building, cheerleading, coaching, connecting, contributing, creating, designing, implementing, intuiting, inventing, leading, listening, logistics, mediating, networking, peacemaking, strategizing, thinking, or something else?

If you find yourself coming up with a long list of Driving Talents, try to narrow it down as much as you can. However, if you can't narrow it down at this point, don't worry – you will hone in on your Driving Talents more in the upcoming lessons.

Play Your Way to Clarity Overview

7. **What one or two Driving Talent(s) emerge(s) in the way you like to play?**

If you need help identifying Driving Talents, please reference page 251.

_____

_____

_____

8. **What parts of your personality come out when you use your Driving Talents?**

Are you generous, loyal, devoted, loving, kind, patient, determined, fair, or optimistic?

_____

_____

_____

BRING MORE PLAY INTO YOUR LIFE

When you reflect on your play, what changes might you want to explore in your work and personal life? How do you want to integrate the missing parts of you and bring them forward? There are usually three possibilities: 1) how you like to play might shed light on your interests, Driving Talents, and personality that you want to draw upon in your career; 2) how you like to play can illuminate how you might bring more fulfillment to your free time; or 3) you might need more free time to play.

As you contemplate this, think about the unmet needs you would like to address through play, both personally and professionally. Now let's look at each of the different ways you might integrate play into your career.

MICHAEL'S STORY: How revisiting play gave him a new career trajectory.

Michael, the twenty-six-year-old sales rep, shared that he grew up in a working-class household. His dad was a plant foreman at a factory, and his mom was a dispatcher at the local police station. Since his parents did not make a lot of money, Michael was on his own the day he turned eighteen.

Michael fell into sales after completing his associate's degree in business. Although he performed satisfactorily at work, he felt unfulfilled, and the work felt unnatural. As an introvert, he didn't feel comfortable selling. What's more, he wasn't able to use his creativity and ingenuity.

He wanted to excel in whatever career he pursued, and he was open to going back to school to complete a bachelor's degree, but only if it was necessary.

When Michael worked through the Inner Compass Process, focusing on play was helpful, because he realized he wasn't using his Driving Talent of building in his job, nor did it reflect his interest in making furniture.

Michael enjoyed building furniture and working with his hands as a child. His interest in his craft continued throughout adulthood. He gifted custom furniture to friends and loved ones for special occasions and sometimes received requests for commissioned projects. Building furniture met Michael's needs for movement, creativity, and craftsmanship.

After completing the Inner Compass Process, Michael decided he would start a business as a furniture maker. It married his Driving Talent of building and his interests in making furniture. It also engaged his independent, creative, and inventive personality.

Michael contacted local furniture stores in the area to share his portfolio. Several of them agreed to place his pieces on display. One store that displayed Michael's furniture was featured in a magazine, and one of his pieces was featured on the cover. Michael's business took off, and he quit his sales job to pursue furniture making full time.

Michael is an excellent example of how play shed light on his interests, Driving Talents and the personality traits he wanted to draw upon in his career.

JOSH'S STORY: How he changed his free time activities to feel more fulfilled.

Josh, the thirty-eight-year-old mortgage broker, had been considering a career change for several years. While he enjoyed his work and made a good income, he felt something was missing. He worked with me to explore other options.

When Josh reviewed the ways he liked to play as a kid, he realized that a large part of his childhood included volunteering for his church. Volunteering gave him a sense of contribution and purpose. As an adult, Josh worked out and spent time with loved ones, but was not actively volunteering.

After completing the Inner Compass Process, Josh remained in the mortgage industry and became involved in his local Rotary Club, which met his need for contribution and purpose. Josh's childhood play illuminated what was missing in his free time now. Josh needed to have a sense of contribution and purpose, and he found he could meet those needs outside of his career.

GRETCHEN'S STORY: How she freed up more time to play and revitalized her life.

Gretchen was a forty-four-year-old management consultant who was married with two children under the age of ten. She was considering a career change, because her job required long hours and her partner complained that she did not spend enough time with the family. Gretchen feared that if she did not make a change, her marriage would fail. However, she was the primary breadwinner, and whatever change she made needed to maintain her income.

When Gretchen explored the way she liked to play, she admitted that she wasn't having any fun and that she was doing chores, running errands, or watching TV in her free time. Gretchen had gotten away from the things she loved to do as a child and from having playtime with her loved ones. Her work-life balance had gotten way off track.

Gretchen grew up in Switzerland and immigrated to the United States with her family when she was twelve. She loved hiking the Alps, biking, and being outdoors as a child. She even shared that it was one reason she fell in love with her husband and moved to the state of Colorado, so they could hike, bike, and spend time outdoors as a family.

Gretchen was the primary breadwinner, so she couldn't leave her job immediately, and because she was at the executive level, her job search might take six to nine months. However, she needed to shift her work-life balance immediately.

Gretchen was terrified to talk to her boss about reducing her hours, not answering calls past 6:00 p.m., and no longer working evenings and weekends. However, after a stressful week at work, she had a courageous conversation with her boss in which she negotiated more parameters around her workweek.

In the short term, Gretchen stopped answering calls after 6:30 p.m. and stopped working on evenings and weekends. This allowed for more time with her family. It took a bit of time for Gretchen to start "playing" again because doing chores after work had become a bad habit for her. She began riding her bike and taking more hikes with her family. As a result, her relationship improved with her partner because their needs for connection and fun were satisfied, and they could rekindle the reason they fell in love in the first place.

Gretchen's job search took ten months, and she eventually transitioned into a chief operations officer position at a small company. Her new job allowed her to spend more time playing and being with her family.

YOUR STORY: HOW WILL YOU CHANGE YOUR LIFE?

Now that you've read all these examples and have done some self-reflection on play, what changes might you want to explore in your work and personal life? Do you want to integrate your interests, Driving Talents, and personality into your career? Do you need to change your roles and responsibilities, work environment, or something else? Perhaps you want to be doing more of what you love in your free time, or you simply need more free time?

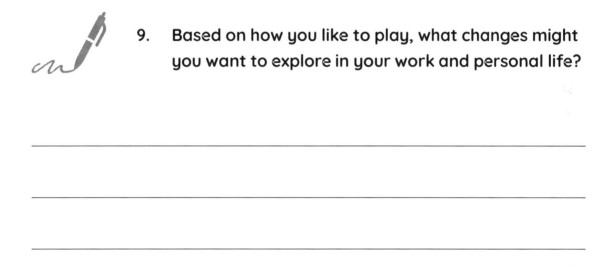

9. Based on how you like to play, what changes might you want to explore in your work and personal life?

___

___

___

10. **If you were to make these changes, what needs would you address, and how would that improve your quality of life?**

For a complete list of needs, please reference page 241.

_____

_____

_____

LESSON 2

YOUR FREEING MINDSET

THROUGH UNPACKING powerful stories from your childhood, you will learn about:

> YOUR FREEING MINDSET: The feelings, thoughts, and behaviors that you associate with being in a state of fulfillment.

You may be reading this book because you don't know what will make you feel fulfilled in your work. Everyone's Freeing Mindset and experience of fulfillment are different because everyone has a different set of needs. This lesson will help you understand what will make you feel fulfilled and what fulfillment feels like for you.

Understanding your Freeing Mindset will help you gauge whether a career is a good fit. When working with clients, I often ask them if a particular career direction would allow for more opportunities to be in their Freeing Mindset. If the answer is yes, we know they're moving in the right direction.

Revisiting times when you experienced your Freeing Mindset will also help you better understand the circumstances that give you a feeling of fulfillment. Just as you did in the last lesson, you will make connections between your happy childhood memories and positive career experiences that illuminate your Driving Talents and your core needs. A career that uses your Driving Talents and meets your core needs is likely to offer more experiences of fulfillment as well.

When you were a small child, you experienced an event or series of events that you interpreted as positive. You formed a story about why the event happened, experienced positive feelings, told yourself positive thoughts, and reacted with behaviors based on that event(s).

You also learned that your needs would be met through that event. Perhaps you enjoyed the connection, safety, security, love, companionship, acknowledgment, or freedom you experienced.

As you grew older, that story became a part of your identity, and if an event happened to you as an adult that you associated as positive, then similar feelings, thoughts, behaviors, and met needs would reemerge.

Mariana, a case manager at Child Protective Services, came to me because she felt stuck in her job and wanted more fulfillment in her career. Mariana entered the field of child protection because she grew up in the foster care system and wanted children to have a better experience than she had. Mariana had been in her role for more than seven years. She disliked the paperwork and wanted to shift out of case management. She was unsure if she wanted to find another position at Child Protective Services or leave the agency altogether.

When I asked Mariana what would make her feel more fulfilled, she answered that she wanted to help people, but she wasn't clear beyond that.

Mariana's favorite memory from childhood was attending summer camp for foster youth. She loved being able to make new friends, participate in fun activities, and just be herself. When I asked her how she felt, what she thought, and how she behaved, she responded, "I felt optimistic and enthusiastic, and thought, *This is the best time ever, and I don't want camp to end*, and I behaved upbeat and energetic."

I also asked Mariana to share a positive memory from her career. Mariana reflected on a time when she worked at a recreation center while she was in college. She enjoyed planning activities and spending time with the staff, and she thought it was a fun job. When I asked her how she felt, what she thought, and how she behaved, she replied, "I felt joyful and enthusiastic and thought, *This is a fun job, and I can be myself*, and I acted upbeat and driven."

When Mariana and I explored the similarities between the memories to help her define her Freeing Mindset, or what fulfillment means to her, she realized she was seeking a mindset of feeling enthusiastic about her work, thinking that she can "be herself," and behaving upbeat and driven. She also recognized that she was able to plan activities in both of her memories and spend time with a community.

Mariana realized how important it was to her to have a job that allowed her to have fun, a quality her current job lacked. She also didn't have enough opportunities to spend time with others in a community in her job. Mariana ended up pivoting her career and accepting a programming position at a local nonprofit that allowed her to plan educational activities for youth and experience more enjoyment.

As you move through this lesson, a big part of your journey will be to explore your stories and how you felt, thought and acted in them. You will define your Freeing Mindset, or what fulfillment means to you based on your stories. Your Freeing Mindset will be unique to you because of your experiences.

You will also begin to understand the circumstances in your life that help you feel fulfilled. Once you can identify those circumstances, you can figure out how to replicate them in your career. In Mariana's story, she needed to be with others in a community. In this lesson, you will read my story and the story of another, client, Mae. Each of us has different circumstances we need to feel fulfilled.

Later in this book, your knowledge of your Freeing Mindset will help you identify jobs, employers and careers that will help you feel fulfilled. You will also be able to determine what might be missing and what actions you can take to be happier at work by asking yourself, "What do I need right now to experience my Freeing Mindset?"

Now let's jump in and identify your Freeing Mindset!

A BLAST TO YOUR PAST

Take some time now to think about a positive or happy memory from childhood. Try to remember the details, such as what happened, who was there, and any other sensations. What did you feel, what did you think, and how did you behave?

Maybe your memory has to do with travel, getting recognized, doing something that you loved, holidays and festivities, travel and adventure, being at a particular place, or being with loved ones.

If you tend to have difficulty recalling things, don't overthink this. Whatever comes to mind, go with it. You cannot get this wrong.

As I mentioned in the introduction, my positive memory from childhood was when I was eight years old and hiked with my parents and sister at Sugarloaf Mountain in Dickerson, Maryland. I remember walking to the top of the summit and picnicking with my family. I felt warmth and connection and thought, *My family loves me.* I talked with my sister, climbed the rock features, and felt present in the world.

Mae, a forty-six-year-old content director at a medical device employer, was referred to me by her human resources department because she seemed to be disengaged from her work. Mae's company wanted to invest in her professional development to retain her as an employee. They were willing to allow her to change her role and responsibilities and choose her projects so that she would remain with the company.

Mae was an only child and had supportive parents growing up. Mae focused on a memory from childhood in which she made imaginary creatures out of pipe cleaners with her best friend. She attached the creatures to her bicycle and rode around all day. Mae felt adventurous and engrossed, and she thought, *Life is full of possibilities, and this is exhilarating.* Mae remembered acting playful and being fully present in the moment.

Now it's your turn. Think back to a positive memory from your childhood. What were you doing? Did you feel friendly, warm, engaged, confident, safe, excited, grateful, inspired, joyful, exhilarated, calm, enlivened, or some other way? When you felt your feelings, what thoughts went through your mind? Lastly, how did you behave? Were you friendly, confident, creative, compassionate, organized, reflective, quiet, sincere, or talkative?

If you have several memories that come to mind, feel free to write all of them down and search for commonalities. Whatever memory or memories you choose, you cannot go wrong because you'll find some quality in them that you're seeking in your career.

1. Share a positive memory from your childhood.

_____

_____

2. How did you feel, think, and behave?

If you need help identifying feelings, please reference page 243; for behaviors, please reference page 245.

_____

_____

NOW

The way you felt, thought, and behaved in your most fulfilled time as a kid is very similar to how you feel, think, and act now when you're satisfied in your career. Take a few minutes to think about a positive or happy memory from your career. Perhaps it was a project you completed, roles and responsibilities assigned to you, an overall job you had, or the relationships you had with your coworkers.

If you have been out of the workforce for some time, or perhaps you have few positive career experiences, you can share a story from volunteering, side hustles, gigs, freelance work, helping a friend or loved one, a creative project that you did at home, or something to that nature.

One of my happiest memories in my career was when I was working as a high school social worker, and I organized a yoga class for my students during our lunch break. The yoga instructor, my students, and I had an incredible bonding experience. I felt connected and openhearted, I thought, *I want to do more of this*, and I acted warm, talkative, and friendly.

Mae reflected on a memory where she was working on a campaign that brought attention to a medical device that she was representing. She enjoyed the work and thought the employer had an admirable mission. She felt engaged and captivated; she thought, *I can tell the stories I want and be creative.* She acted productive and engaged.

Now it's your turn. Think back to a positive memory of your career. What happened? Did you feel appreciative, calm, clear-headed, friendly, engaged, confident, excited, inspired, joyful, empowered, or some other way? When you felt your feelings, what thoughts went through your mind? Lastly, how did you behave? Were you friendly, driven, enthusiastic, passionate, confident, creative, compassionate, organized, reflective, talkative, or something else?

If you have several memories that come to mind, feel free to experiment with them and explore the commonalities.

3. Share a positive memory from your career.

_____

_____

_____

4. How did you think, feel, and behave?

If you need help identifying feelings, please reference page 243; for behaviors, please reference page 245.

_____

_____

_____

CONNECTING THE DOTS

Most people's positive career experiences closely mirror their positive memories as a child. Perhaps the feelings were similar, the thoughts had parallel themes, and/or the behaviors were identical. What do your positive memories of childhood and your career have in common?

My memories share the theme of connection. I felt connected to my family in my childhood memory and my students in my adult memory. My thoughts were of love and acceptance. My behaviors mirrored each other in that I acted warm, talkative, and friendly.

Mae's memories shared feelings of engagement and adventure. Her thoughts were similar in that they focused on the joy of the moment. She realized that she behaves playfully and is present when she's in her "happy place" because of her needs for creativity, inspiration, and adventure.

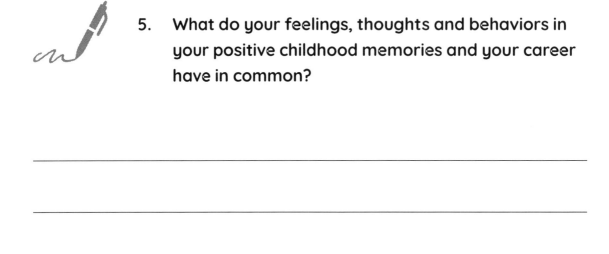

5. **What do your feelings, thoughts and behaviors in your positive childhood memories and your career have in common?**

_____

_____

_____

Just as your feelings, thoughts and behaviors in your childhood memory mirror those of your career memory, the *circumstances* that created those feelings, thoughts and actions are likely similar as well.

My childhood memory stands out because it was the first memory I have of my family hiking together. It was a novel experience, and I was surrounded by people I loved. When I created a yoga class for my high school students, many had never done yoga before. In both experiences, I was surrounded by people who accepted me, doing something new and different. Having my own business allows me the freedom to create novel experiences for my clients and arrange my schedule to have time outside of work for novel experiences.

In Mae's childhood memory of riding her bike around with her pipe-cleaner animals, she was free to explore and share her creative ideas. Similarly, in her positive memory of her career, she was free to create the campaign using her creativity and ingenuity. In both experiences, freedom to create was a needed circumstance for her to thrive.

Now it's your turn. What do the circumstances in your memories have in common? These are also circumstances you need to thrive at work.

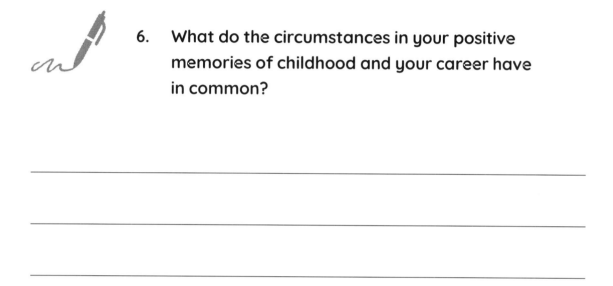

6. What do the circumstances in your positive memories of childhood and your career have in common?

_____

_____

_____

YOUR TRUE NORTH GUIDE

Take a few moments to look at the patterns between your childhood and adulthood memories and write a definition of your Freeing Mindset *now*, including your feelings, thoughts, and behaviors when you are in a state of fulfillment.

When I'm in my Freeing Mindset, I feel connected and a sense of belonging, I think, *I'm loved and connected to those around me*, and I behave warm, friendly, and talkative.

When Mae is in her Freeing Mindset, she feels engaged and creative. She thinks, *I can tell the stories I want and be creative*. She acts productive and engaged.

What is your Freeing Mindset now? How do you feel, what do you think, and how do you behave?

If you notice that you have several patterns that describe what fulfillment means to you, then write several versions of your Freeing Mindset. You cannot get this wrong!

7. Write your Freeing Mindset based on your reflections and add it to your True North Guide (page 18).

I feel:

I think:

I behave:

NEEDS

My positive experiences met my needs for belonging and connection. Mae's positive memories met her needs for creativity and adventure.

When you look at your positive memories from childhood, what needs were fulfilled? For example, if your positive memory from childhood included happy memories with your family and friends, perhaps you learned that your need for connection, love, support, and safety would be met. If your positive memory from childhood was of being recognized, given an award, or something of that nature, your need to be seen and heard may have been honored. If your positive memory was of an adventure or trip, perhaps your needs for autonomy and freedom were appeased.

8. **What needs were satisfied in your positive memories?**

For a complete list of needs, please reference page 241.

_____

_____

_____

YOUR DRIVING TALENTS

As mentioned in the last lesson, **your Driving Talents are your innate abilities that help you feel fulfilled at work**. While you may be good at a lot of things, **your Driving Talents are the one or two abilities that seem to just flow for you and that make you feel fulfilled**. They aren't just talents but lifelong traits that can be traced back to your childhood stories

Your positive memories can help you further clarify your Driving Talent(s). There are three particular ways you might uncover your Driving Talents when you look back to your positive or happy memories of childhood: 1) your Driving Talent is connected to your core needs; 2) you were likely doing something that came naturally to you; 3) the person you were with had a quality that you admired and took on as your own.

Your core needs became your Driving Talents.

I'm a strong example of my core need becoming my Driving Talent. In both my happy memories of childhood and my career, my needs for belonging and connection were fulfilled. In my childhood memory, I connected with my family in the mountains. In my career memory, I created programs to help students connect with themselves and one another. My Driving Talent is connecting, which I define as helping individuals connect with themselves and one another.

I value connection, and I'm a talented connector.

Can you see a strong connection between your needs and your Driving Talents? If so, what's the connection?

You were using your Driving Talent in your positive memories of childhood and in your career.

Mae is an excellent example of doing what comes naturally to her and motivates her, both in her happy childhood and career memories. In her childhood memory, she created pipe-cleaner creatures from her imagination and went on an adventure with her friend. Mae's favorite memory in her career was when she worked on a marketing campaign. She was doing what comes naturally to her in both her positive memories—using her imagination to create.

What were you doing in your positive memories? Were you using your Driving Talents? If so, how?

A person in your positive memories of childhood or in your career had a Driving Talent that you admired and took on as your own.

Diana, a fifty-three-year-old stay-at-home mom, did the Inner Compass Process because her children had gone off to college and she had a desire for meaningful work.

She grew up in rural Indiana, and her family struggled with poverty and homelessness. She went to community college to study bookkeeping. Diana pursued bookkeeping because she did not want to experience poverty ever again.

Diana met her husband at a holiday party for a company where she had worked as a bookkeeper and he worked in the marketing department. They married and decided that she would stay at home because his career had taken off. They agreed that Diana would care for the children and the family finances because she enjoyed bookkeeping and investing.

Diana shared a positive memory of being mentored by her middle school guidance counselor, because she did not have much support at home. She would meet with her guidance counselor weekly, which got her through the toughest times at home.

One of Diana's happiest memories in her career was volunteering to teach financial classes at the local women's shelter and mentoring others. She described her Driving Talent as advising or supporting others to help them meet their needs.

Diana's Driving Talent of advising and supporting others was a quality that she admired in her guidance counselor and took on as her own.

Do your positive memories of childhood bring out a person whose traits you emulate with your Driving Talents? Who is that person, and what qualities do you emulate?

Now, using the insights from the sections above, write down some notes about your one or two Driving Talent(s). What Driving Talent(s) is/are illuminated when you look back to your positive memories? Are you talented at advising, analyzing, building, cheerleading, coaching, connecting, contributing, creating, designing, implementing, intuiting, inventing, leading, listening, logistics, mediating, networking, peacemaking, strategizing, thinking, or something else? Remember, when you identify your Driving Talent, make sure it brings you a sense of fulfillment and that you feel more alive when using it.

If your Driving Talent repeats from the previous lesson, that is expected.

9. What one or two Driving Talent(s) have you developed because of your positive memories? What is your simple definition of it/them?

If you need help identifying Driving Talents, please reference page 251.

_____

_____

_____

BRING MORE FULFILLMENT INTO YOUR LIFE

When you reflect on your Freeing Mindset, what changes might you want to explore in your work and personal life? Do you want to shift some of your roles and responsibilities? Do you perhaps need a different work environment or culture? What conditions have you identified that you need to thrive at work?

I know that I need to connect with clients and colleagues in ways that are novel and meaningful to me. I love using my Driving Talents of creating and connecting to produce experiences such as workshops, retreats, and courses that are deep, reflective, and connective. I experience warmth, joy, and engagement when I do; I'm in a mindset I desire.

As mentioned, Mae's employer paid for her career coaching because they hoped to retain her as an employee. After researching different job options, Mae decided she wanted to remain as a content director for her current employer.

Mae needed to make an internal shift, because her job already provided the conditions she needed to thrive. She brainstormed ways to bring more inspiration to her current projects and also enrolled in several storytelling workshops to get her creative juices flowing. Mae concluded that she needed to reinvent her mindset by bringing more storytelling elements to the way she created content. She also needed to choose the projects that interested her so that she could remain engaged with her work.

10. Based on your Freeing Mindset, what changes might you want to explore in your work and personal life?

LESSON 3

YOUR BINDING MINDSET

BINDING MINDSET OVERVIEW

> Your Binding Mindset consists of the feelings, thoughts, and behaviors that you associate with being in a state of unfulfillment.

First, we used positive memories from your childhood to help you understand your Freeing Mindset. Now, we will focus on your Binding Mindset, or the feelings, thoughts, and behaviors that you associate with being in a state of unfulfillment, by exploring a negative or unhappy memory.

Understanding your Binding Mindset will help you recognize when you're in a state of unfulfillment so that you can more easily shift out of it. You will also better understand the circumstances that lead to unfulfillment, which will further clarify your career search.

When you were a small child, something happened to you that you experienced as negative. This could include losing a loved one, being bullied, experiencing your parents getting a divorce, or any formative event in your life. You formed a story about why it happened and experienced feelings, thoughts, and behaviors based on that event(s).

As you grew older, that story became a part of your identity. If something happened to you as an adult that you perceived as negative, those same feelings, thoughts, and behaviors might reemerge. Your initial reactions, like withdrawing or acting out, may have snowballed into more destructive behaviors like isolation or manipulation.

Sigmund Freud, an Austrian neurologist and psychoanalyst in the early 1900s, called this repetition compulsion. It is the idea that people fall into patterns because they become ingrained and familiar to us, even if they don't serve us. It's why people stay in unhealthy relationships or careers that don't serve them. It's also why the same arguments come up again and again, and why you may struggle at work even when there's nothing wrong with your external circumstances. Freud's research formed the foundation for cognitive behavioral therapy, attachment theory, and habit formation research.

Clinical research suggests that that repetition compulsion is a function of how our brain works.

The brain is made of approximately 100 billion nerve cells called neurons.[2] Neurons have the incredible ability to transmit electrochemical signals over long distances and send messages to each other. A neural pathway is formed when the same messages are sent repeatedly; hence, some of the behaviors associated with repetition compulsion can be explained on a cellular level. Neural pathways play a role in reinforcing all habits and behaviors that we repeat, not just bad habits and/or maladaptive cognition and behavior.

This phenomenon is why you experience similar feelings, thoughts, and behaviors whenever you are triggered and uncomfortable.

Rohan, a data analyst, shared a series of unhappy childhood memories of being scolded by his father. Rohan grew up in Mumbai, India, and attended a college preparatory school. His father ran a successful business and was always traveling for work.

As a child, Rohan desperately wanted to spend quality time with his father, but his father went straight into the home office after returning from his business trips.

Rohan had a clear memory of his excitement at his father's return from a business trip. When he greeted his father, he was immediately reprimanded for receiving a B in his mathematics class. This is just one example of his father's critical and demanding personality.

Rohan needed respect, understanding, and approval, but his father gave him criticism instead. He remembered feeling sad and ashamed and thinking, *I'm not good enough*. He initially wanted to please his father, but he eventually began withdrawing, becoming perfectionistic, and avoiding his dad because he didn't want to deal with the criticism.

Rohan admitted that even as an adult, he struggled when his work mistakes were pointed out. When this happened, he would think *I'm not good enough* and feel sad and frustrated. He also isolated himself in his office so he could focus. He didn't want any interruptions, because he feared they would affect the quality of his work. Even though he was in a supportive work environment, repetition compulsion led him to experience these negative thoughts, feelings, and behaviors.

Rohan hired me because he thought he needed to change companies in order to receive a promotion. As part of the Inner Compass Process, he approached his manager to ask her why he wasn't being promoted.

His manager told him that people perceived him as being aloof and unfriendly because he often kept his door closed, ended conversations abruptly, and seemed to want to get people out of his office as quickly as possible. Despite all this, she deeply respected him because of his high-quality work. Before their conversation, Rohan hadn't even realized that she respected him. Rohan's mindset was preventing him from accepting the respect and approval he so desperately needed.

While it was hard to hear, her feedback helped him better understand what was going on.

Rohan learned how to recognize his feelings of extreme perfectionism and to counter them. He started using "The Work of Byron Katie", an inquiry practice, to support him with countering his negative thoughts.[3]

Rohan began opening his door and building relationships with other employees. He also asked for the opportunity to supervise a team, a role that would allow him to determine if he liked managing others. After demonstrating his capability to manage complex projects and lead a team, he was eventually promoted to a project manager eight months after completing career coaching.

While Rohan's perfectionism initially hindered his relationships at work, it also contributed to his Driving Talent of finding patterns and analyzing situations. His Driving Talent helped him shift into a better position at work because he could analyze what was going on and create a better outcome for himself.

Just as Rohan was able to make many positive changes in his career due to recognizing his Binding Mindset, exploring your Binding Mindset will help you understand why you are stuck so that you can make changes. These may be internal or external changes, depending on your unique situation. You will also recognize the Driving Talents you've developed because of your Binding Mindset.

A BLAST TO YOUR PAST

A warning before you begin this exercise. Some people have unresolved trauma connected to their childhood memories. If you know that revisiting childhood memories is triggering or emotionally unsafe for you, please stop this lesson and process these experiences with a licensed therapist. You can also skip this lesson altogether.

Take some time now to think about a negative or unhappy memory from childhood. It may have been an experience of being bullied, the death of a loved one, a difficult transition, an injury, struggles in school, a disagreement with a friend, or cases of abuse or neglect. It was something that shut you down. Any memory will work.

If multiple stories come to mind, please summarize the overall experience or write down multiple memories and search for commonalities.

My unhappy memory is when I was bullied in the fourth grade. Three girls taped a thumbtack on my chair. My teacher reprimanded the girls, but ultimately, did nothing to protect me. She didn't even acknowledge my feelings. I remember feeling angry, sad, and alone, and thinking, *No one likes me, and no one ever will.* I initially responded by going out to the playground and acting clingy or trying to hang out with the girls when they didn't want me there. I never processed that experience into my teen years, and as a result, primarily during middle and high school, I became withdrawn and judgmental of myself and others.

Another memory was at a summer camp in the fifth grade. A boy teased me because I dressed androgynously and had short hair. I yelled at the boy to protect myself from his teasing, and he pinned me up against the fence and threatened to beat me up. I remember feeling angry, sad and frustrated and thinking, *No one likes me, and he embarrassed me in front of others*. I pretended that nothing had happened, held the embarrassment within, and experienced self-critical thoughts.

When I compared these memories, they both carried the feelings of anger and sadness, the thoughts of people disliking me, and the behaviors of acting like nothing ever happened, clinginess, and self-criticism.

Matthew was a twenty-eight-year-old legal assistant who hated his job. He grew up wanting approval from his father, a well-known attorney who had risen to the top of his field. Matthew believed that his father never really understood him. When Matthew tinkered with computers as a preteen and showed his accomplishments to his father, his father dismissed him. His father only paid attention to him when he asked about his father's work.

When Matthew reflected on his relationship with his father, he felt discouraged and hurt and thought, *Why doesn't he see me?* He also became withdrawn. As Matthew turned into a teenager, he would seek approval from those around him, even if it was detrimental to his other needs.

Now it's your turn. Think back to a negative memory of your childhood. Did you feel afraid, frustrated, angry, confused, worried, disconnected, uneasy, lonely, heartbroken, depressed, nervous, helpless, or some other way? When you felt these feelings, what thoughts went through your mind? Lastly, how did you behave? Were you aggressive, avoidant, careless, rude, guarded, inconsiderate, judgmental, critical, manipulative, withdrawn, or something else? Did your initial reactions snowball into long-lasting behaviors? If so, how?

1. Share a negative or unhappy memory of your childhood.

2. How did you feel, think, and behave initially? How did your behaviors transition over time?

If you need help identifying feelings, please reference page 247; for behaviors, please reference page 249.

NOW

The way you felt, thought, and behaved in your most unfulfilled time as a kid is similar to how you feel, think, and act now when you're unfulfilled in your career. Take a few minutes to think about a negative memory from your career. Perhaps it was a project that went poorly, roles and responsibilities that were misaligned, a job you disliked, or a rocky relationship with a boss.

If you haven't been in the workforce for some time, you can share a story about a terrible volunteer experience, a project that was a disaster, a relationship that went sour, a gig or side hustle that was a bust, or something to that nature.

As with the previous section, know your boundaries and take care of yourself when doing this exercise. If you experienced workplace trauma, please process this experience with a licensed therapist or skip this section.

My unhappy memory from my career was when I joined a business networking group to grow my business. After three to four months of involvement, I did not create any strong connections with the other business owners. I felt disconnected and alone and thought, *I don't fit in here,* and wavered between acting clingy or withdrawn.

Matthew admitted that he did not feel good at his job as a legal assistant and that it did not come naturally to him—he was only doing it for his father's approval. When he felt depressed and frustrated, he thought, *I'm not good at this. Is being a lawyer my only option? What if my parents disapprove of my path?* He acted quiet and subdued. He shared that he probably didn't seem enthusiastic about his work unless working on technical issues.

Now it's your turn. Think back to a negative memory from your career. Did you feel concerned, frustrated, irritated, confused, worried, disconnected, uneasy, lonely, alarmed, depressed, nervous, vulnerable, or some other way? When you felt these feelings, what thoughts went through your mind? Lastly, how did you behave? Were you annoyed, impatient, avoidant, careless, indifferent, jealous, inconsiderate, judgmental, critical, manipulative, withdrawn, or something else?

3. Share a negative or unhappy memory from your career.

_____

_____

_____

4. How did you think, feel, and behave?

If you need help identifying feelings, please reference page 247; for behaviors, please reference page 249.

_____

_____

_____

CONNECTING THE DOTS

Most people's negative career experiences closely mirror their unhappy memories as a child. Perhaps the feelings were similar, the thoughts had parallel themes, or the behaviors mirrored each other. What do your unhappy memories of childhood and your career have in common?

My memories shared the theme of feeling lonely and disconnected and thoughts that people didn't like me or I don't fit in. My behaviors mirrored each other in that I acted clingy, withdrawn, and self-critical.

Matthew's memories shared the feelings of discouragement, thoughts of not being good enough, and withdrawal and approval-seeking behaviors.

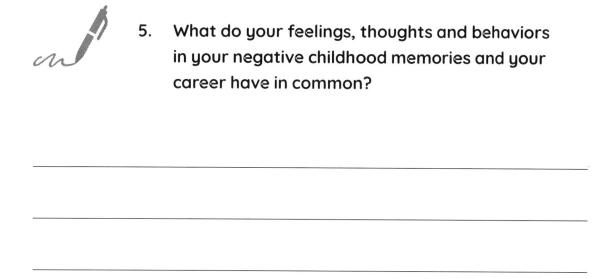

5. What do your feelings, thoughts and behaviors in your negative childhood memories and your career have in common?

_____

_____

_____

In the last lesson, you identified which circumstances are present when you experience your Freeing Mindset. Now we're going to look at commonalities between the circumstances in your negative experiences.

In my memory of being bullied in fourth grade, I was hurt by my classmates and wanted to fit in. Since there were only six girls in my elementary school class, there were not enough kids for me to connect with to find my tribe. My career memory has very similar conditions in that I wanted to fit in with the other business owners and did not feel a sense of connection and belonging. I eventually left the business networking group and joined another, where I thought I had more in common with the other business owners.

In Matthew's childhood memory, his father didn't value the things that interested Matthew. In his adult memory, he was in a job that didn't use his Driving Talents. Because he was hired to be a legal assistant, his employers expected him to focus on secretarial duties instead of his advanced computer skills. He was surrounded by people who didn't value the skills he wanted to use in both memories.

Do you see yourself in Matthew's story? His story demonstrates a pattern I've seen with many of my clients. In trying to make other people happy, they choose positions that activate their Binding Mindsets. The problem is, even if someone else, such as your spouse or parent, is satisfied with your job, if you're in a position that doesn't allow you to thrive, you won't feel fulfilled. That's why I'm so grateful you're reading this book — so that you can choose a job that will be fulfilling for you.

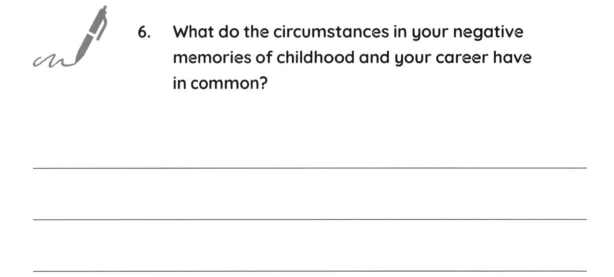

6. What do the circumstances in your negative memories of childhood and your career have in common?

_____

_____

_____

YOUR TRUE NORTH GUIDE

Take a few moments to look at the patterns between your childhood and adulthood memories and write a definition of your Binding Mindset *now*, including your feelings, thoughts, and behaviors when you are in a state of unfulfillment.

When I'm in my Binding Mindset, I feel disconnected and sad, I think, *I don't belong*, and I behave clingy, withdrawn, or judgmental of myself and others.

When Matthew was in his Binding Mindset, he felt depressed and frustrated, he thought, *I'm not good at this, but I want their approval*, and he acted quiet and subdued.

When you're in your Binding Mindset, how do you feel, what do you think, and how do you behave?

7. Write your Binding Mindset based on your reflections and add it to your True North Guide (page 18).

I feel:

I think:

I behave:

YOUR BINDING MINDSET AND YOUR CORE NEEDS

When I thought back on my negative memories, my needs for belonging, connection, and safety were not met. When Matthew reflected on his negative memories, his needs for support and approval were not satisfied.

When you look at your negative memories from childhood, what needs were unfulfilled? For example, if your negative memories included a lack of support from your family and peers, perhaps you learned that your need for connection, love, support, and safety would be dissatisfied. If your negative memories involved being ignored, or criticized, or something of that nature, your need to be seen and heard may have been dishonored. If your negative memory lacked choice, perhaps your needs for autonomy and freedom were undermined.

8. When you explore your unhappy memories from childhood and adulthood, what needs weren't being met?

For a complete list of needs, please reference page 241.

_____

_____

_____

FROM YOUR DEEPEST PAIN TO YOUR DRIVING TALENTS

Your Driving Talents are your one or two innate abilities that motivate you and help you feel fulfilled at work. While you likely have many *talents*, your *Driving* Talents are the one or two abilities that make you feel satisfied.

You can uncover your Driving Talents by looking at what you did to meet your needs in your painful moments. If you look closely at your unhappy memories, you will find your deep longing to have your needs met. That desire fueled you to develop your innate strengths, or your Driving Talents, even further.

For example, in both my unhappy memories of being bullied in childhood and not fitting in during adulthood, I longed for belonging and connection with others. In my pursuit to meet this deep need, I observed my peers to try to figure out how to get them to like me. While this desire to be liked manifested itself as clinginess as a kid, it also helped me become highly attuned to myself and others, which has developed my Driving Talent of connecting.

In Matthew's unhappy memory of seeking his father's approval in childhood, he had a deep need for support and approval that wasn't met. As a result, he strategized and tried different things to win his father's approval. This reveals his Driving Talent for strategizing, which he uses in his current work as a computer network engineer. Matthew defined strategizing as his ability to solve problems, especially with technology.

Matthew already had the innate ability to strategize, and in trying to meet his unmet needs, he was forced to develop it further. The same goes for you – your Driving Talents are innate, and you likely developed them further in trying to meet your deepest needs.

What Driving Talents have you developed because of your Binding Mindset? Are you talented at advising, analyzing, building, cheerleading, coaching, connecting, contributing, creating, designing, implementing, intuiting, inventing, leading, listening, logistics, mediating, networking, peacemaking, strategizing, thinking, or something else?

Remember, when you identify your Driving Talent, make sure it brings you a sense of fulfillment and that you feel more alive when using it.

If your Driving Talent repeats from the previous lesson, that is normal and supposed to happen.

9. **What one or two Driving Talent(s) have you developed because of your negative memories? What is your simple definition of it/them?**

If you need help identifying Driving Talents, please reference page 251.

_____

_____

_____

HOW TO SHIFT OUT OF YOUR BINDING MINDSET

As we've just seen, understanding your Binding Mindset can help you uncover your Driving Talents. Knowing how you feel, think, and behave when you're in your bind is also helpful in shifting out of it more quickly.

To shift out of your bind, you must first gain awareness. Then do the opposite of what your Binding Mindset inclines you to do.[4]

Here are some examples of how to shift out of a Binding Mindset. Doing the opposite of your Binding Mindset isn't typically easy because of repetition compulsion. Your brain has been shaped to fall into the patterns of your Binding Mindset. You will need to train yourself to create new neural pathways. Lean on the support of others and be patient with yourself. You can do it!

If your Binding Mindset is to isolate, reach out to others.

If you feel alone, and want to isolate, distance yourself, shut down, or hide, reach out to others and connect.

Matthew withdrew from others when he was in his Binding Mindset. He enlisted the help of a therapist to support him in speaking up for himself. He also reconnected with his middle and high school friends who pursued tech careers for support in making a career change.

If your Binding Mindset is to measure yourself against others, practice kindness and humility toward yourself and others.

If you measure yourself against others, and find yourself being critical, judgmental, or opinionated, shift instead to practicing kindness and humility toward yourself and others.

When I'm in my Binding Mindset, my fear turns into judging and criticizing others. When I notice myself shifting into my Binding Mindset, I have learned to give myself a lot of self-love and empathy. Self-love puts me at ease and then I'm able to be more kind and humble toward others as well.

If your Binding Mindset is to lose motivation, take action instead.

If you procrastinate or lose motivation, you need to act. It may feel very difficult to do anything, but you can shift out of inaction by taking one small step and then another. Think of one simple task you can do to move forward, and then do that. As you take small actions, you will feel yourself shifting out of your Binding Mindset and feeling better. You can then create a plan of action and begin executing it.

When another client of mine was in his Binding Mindset, he tended not to take action in his job search. He countered his Binding Mindset by creating a schedule to apply for positions, working with a job search accountability partner, and setting goals and timelines to make the change.

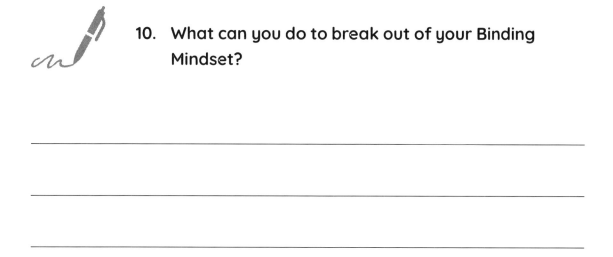

10. What can you do to break out of your Binding Mindset?

_____

_____

_____

Your Freeing and Binding Mindsets are opposites, as are the circumstances behind them.

Did you notice that your Freeing and Binding Mindsets are almost total opposites? Your Freeing Mindset indicates how you feel, think and act when you are fulfilled and your needs are met; your Binding Mindset indicates how you feel, think and act when you are unfulfilled and your needs aren't met. Unsurprisingly, the circumstances that foster your Freeing Mindset and activate your Binding Mindset are also opposites.

Because your needs, Driving Talents, and innate personality remain the same, your Freeing Mindset and Binding Mindset are like opposite sides of the same coin.

My Freeing Mindset is fostered by circumstances when I'm with people who accept me and when I'm doing something new and novel. When I'm in my Freeing Mindset, I feel connected and a sense of belonging, I think, *I'm loved and connected to those around me*, and I behave warm, friendly, and talkative.

My Binding Mindset is activated when I'm in situations in which I don't feel accepted or connected to the people around me. When I'm in my Binding Mindset, I feel disconnected and sad, I think, *I don't belong*, and I behave withdrawn or critical of myself and others.

You don't need to look very closely to see that my Freeing and Binding Mindsets land on opposite ends of the continuum of how connected I feel. At one end of the spectrum (my Freeing Mindset), I feel totally connected. At the other (my Binding Mindset), I feel disconnected.

Now let's look at the Freeing and Binding Mindsets of Mae, the forty-six-year-old content director at a medical device employer from the last lesson.

Mae is in her Freeing Mindset when she can be creative and use her imagination. When she is in her Freeing Mindset, Mae feels engaged and creative. She thinks, *I can tell the stories I want and be creative*. She acts productive and engaged.

Situations in which Mae has tight restrictions or cannot freely express herself activate her Binding Mindset. When Mae is in her bind, she feels disinterested and bored. She thinks, *I can't express myself or create the way I want to*. She acts disengaged and disinterested.

While my spectrum is based on connection, Mae's is based on creative freedom. When she can have a lot of creative freedom, she experiences her Freeing Mindset. When she is restricted, she goes into her Binding Mindset.

What about you? Are your Freeing and Binding Mindsets total opposites?

BRING MORE FULFILLMENT TO YOUR LIFE

When you reflect on your unhappy memories, how does it make you want to change your work or personal life? Do you want to change who you work with, what you do, or how you do it? Perhaps you want to add more self-care in your free time. Or maybe you want to do some work to get out of your bind when it comes up.

There is no right answer. Trust yourself and your intuition to write what makes sense for you.

Doing this work helped me see that My Binding Mindset is activated when I'm not self- connected or connected with others. As a result, I intentionally give myself acceptance and love when I'm in networking situations where I think I don't belong. I've also had to be patient in finding my tribe and trying multiple networking groups until I found one where I felt accepted and connected.

I also know that I need to have projects that allow me to be creative and connect with my tribe; otherwise, I feel isolated and shift into my Binding Mindset. I regularly collaborate with companies, associations, and schools so that I have collaboration and creativity in my work.

Matthew realized that his work as a legal assistant was putting him in a bind because his employers didn't value his Driving Talents. He needed to be doing work that he enjoyed, used his Driving Talents, and made him feel competent. As a preteen, Matthew had tinkered with computers, and as an adult, he enjoyed tech assignments. He changed careers into network administration while working with a therapist to support him through healing from his relationship with his father.

11. Based on your Binding Mindset, what changes might you want to explore in your work and personal life?

_____

_____

_____

LESSON 4

YOUR CORE VALUES

THINK BACK TO THE STORIES you told in the last three lessons. In each of them, you identified your needs.

You likely noticed yourself writing down the same needs over and over again. The needs that you've written down repeatedly in the last sections aren't just your needs – they are your values.

> Your values are your needs that are most important to you, that you have prioritized above all others.

Your needs might change over time, but your values stay consistent.

For example, Rachel, a program director in higher education, felt burned out and frustrated working over seventy-five hours a week in a thankless job. She pursued career coaching with me because she wanted to love her job again but was unsure about her options outside of higher education.

When Rachel was a child, she loved roaming rural Minnesota woods and discovering new trails. She was always outside or reading adventure books. The needs she met through play were *spontaneity* and *freedom*.

When I asked about her happiest childhood memories, she shared a story of her family taking a trip to Minneapolis and visiting the art museum. It was very different from her day to day life in rural Minnesota, and she loved the newness of being in the city. It met her needs for *growth* and *freedom*.

Her positive career memory was developing a university program for students to connect and reflect on their experiences abroad. Her supervisor gave her a lot of autonomy and freedom to create the program. The needs she satisfied in her positive career memory were *community, growth, freedom,* and *appreciation*.

When Rachel was eight years old, her family abruptly moved to Fargo and away from the woods and trails she loved. She was also forced to move away from her friends. Her needs for *spontaneity, freedom,* and *community* were no longer served in her new home.

Her negative memory of her career was working with a new supervisor who changed her role to focus solely on case management. She was no longer able to create innovative programs or experience autonomy in her work. Her needs for *freedom, growth, appreciation*, and *community* were no longer fulfilled.

By telling her stories, Rachel recognized her core values as being *spontaneity, freedom, growth, community* and *appreciation*.

YOUR CHILDLIKE DEFINITIONS OF YOUR VALUES CLARIFY WHAT'S IMPORTANT TO YOU.

As adults, we tend to overthink things and make them too complicated. I always ask my clients to write down their childlike definitions of their values because it keeps them simple and straightforward.

Rachel's childlike definitions of her values are:
- Spontaneity: I can have fun and try something new.

- Freedom: I can choose what I want to do.
- Growth: I can learn something new and develop as a person.
- Community: I always have someone to go to when I need it, and people need me, too.

Appreciation: I brighten your day just because I'm me, and you brighten my day just because you're you.

Rachel found that by sharing her values, she rediscovered a lost part of herself. Rachel had disconnected from her values while working with her current employer. She initially shared more values with the university when she started her job, but the administration changed over fourteen years, and it was no longer a good fit. The exercise of identifying her values was critical for Rachel in realizing that she wasn't in alignment with her work. She wasn't having fun, she wasn't growing in her role, and she did not have the support she desired from the administration.

Rachel left higher education and pivoted into programming for a company that organized employment opportunities and internships for college students. She felt more aligned with her values at her new company, as they allowed her to have more flexibility and freedom to design unique experiences for students. She also felt that her values of freedom and appreciation aligned with her coworkers because she could be herself, joke around, and have fun.

If your work culture does not permit you to work within your values, you will feel like your inner compass is not calibrated. You may feel like you're swimming upstream or don't fit in with your coworkers or supervisors.

For example, if you value freedom, but your work doesn't provide the flexibility you need, you may feel stifled and frustrated. If you value autonomy but have a micromanaging boss, you may feel constrained. On the flip side, if you value connection but your boss is completely hands-off, you likely will feel unsupported. Any of these circumstances may be enough of a reason to leave your job. This is why it's so important to understand your values.

A disconnect in values can also make you question yourself and activate your

Binding Mindset. When your job doesn't meet your values, you might think that there's something wrong with you, and wonder why you can't just go with the flow or accept your circumstances, when in reality, you just have a different set of values than your workplace. When you understand your values and how important they are, it's easier to accept yourself and find a work culture that shares your values. This synergy between you and your workplace will provide more opportunities for you to experience your Freeing Mindset.

Just like Rachel, you will be identifying your core values during this lesson. You will also be recognizing your needs now based on your life circumstances. This newfound awareness will help you clarify if your current employer is a good fit and the values necessary to you in your work moving forward.

A BLAST TO YOUR PAST

Your most important needs have formed your core values. Your stories from childhood illuminate these needs because they were satisfied in your stories of your Freeing Mindset, and not satisfied in your stories of your Binding Mindset.

When I played as a kid by riding my bike outside, hiking, going on adventures, making art projects and attending art classes, I met my needs for *connection, engagement, novelty, creativity,* and *community.*

In my positive memories of going hiking with my family for the first time and organizing a yoga class for high school kids, my needs for *belonging, novelty,* and *connection* were appeased.

When I was bullied as a kid and had a negative experience of networking as an adult, my unmet needs were *safety, connection, acceptance,* and *belonging*.

When I reflect on my most important needs in my memories, I can see that *connection, belonging, creativity,* and *novelty* form my set of core values.

My "childlike" definitions of my values are:
- Connection: I want to get to know and spend time with you.
- Belonging: I want you to like me.

- Creativity: I like to build things.
- Novelty: I like trying new things.

Diana, a fifty-three-year-old stay-at-home mom who was mentioned in Lesson 2, shared that she loved playing with her younger siblings as a child, jumping in the mud, and pretending she was a shopkeeper as a child. Her play satisfied her needs for *security, mentorship,* and *gratitude.*

Diana had a positive memory of being mentored by her middle school guidance counselor because she did not have much support at home. She shared that she would meet with her guidance counselor weekly, which got her through the most challenging times at home. One of Diana's happiest memories in her career was volunteering to teach financial classes at the local women's shelter and mentoring others. Her positive experiences met her needs for *mentorship, security, gratitude,* and *contribution.*

Diana grew up with an abusive father who suffered from alcoholism and an emotionally unavailable mother. As a result, her needs for *security, mentorship,* and *safety* weren't fulfilled. Diana's negative adult memory happened when she was volunteering at her kids' school. Another volunteer disagreed with Diana's opinion in a meeting and became verbally abusive in front of all other volunteers. She felt unsafe, and her needs for *security, safety, a*nd *trust* weren't satisfied.

When Diana was asked to reflect on her core values based on her memories, she decided on mentorship, security, gratitude, and contribution. Her "childlike" definitions of her values were:
- Mentorship: The giving and receiving of support and love.
- Security: I have what I need, and all my needs are provided for.
- Gratitude: I'm thankful for what I have and the people who care for me.
- Contribution: I want to make a difference for others like my mentor did for me.

Now it's your turn. What are your needs from the memories you revisited in the last three lessons? After you write down your core values, write a simple, childlike definition for each of them.

THE INNER COMPASS PROCESS

 1. **What are your top four values from your memories? Define them using a simple "childlike" definition and add them to your True North Guide (page 18).**

Please reference pages 31 (Play), 49 (Freeing Mindset), and 64 (Binding Mindset) to see what you wrote down.

MY VALUE	MY DEFINITION

NOW
What are your needs?

To make a meaningful change, in addition to honoring your values, you must honor your needs here and now. I don't believe your career is meant to meet all your needs, but I do want your career to meet more of them.

What you need in your twenties will look different from what you need in your thirties, forties, fifties, and sixties.

I started my business in my early thirties because of my need for flexibility and more financial security (social work didn't pay much). Now, I have shifted to needing more joy and community connection, so I've taken a part-time job as a college counselor at the high school I attended.

Diana pursued a career in financial counseling for military families in her fifties because of her needs for meaning and purpose. Diana's children had left for college, and she wanted to use her time in a way that felt like she was giving back to others.

Take a minute to think about your needs at this moment in your life. Do you need appreciation, autonomy, beauty, belonging, choice, communication, community, connection, contribution, freedom, fun, harmony, honesty, humor, independence, learning, meaning, nurturance, peace, physical safety, security, self-expression trust, well-being, or something else?

2. **What are your needs now? Add them to your True North Guide (page 18).**

If you need help identifying your needs, please reference page 241.

_____

_____

_____

WHY MIGHT YOU BE STUCK?

People are often hard on themselves for staying stuck in a job, career, employer, or industry that no longer serves them, or they remain unemployed or underemployed. Remember, when you made your choice, regardless of the outcome, a deep need motivated you.

Anna, a forty-two-year-old compliance manager at an aerospace company, shared that she had been considering a career change for almost seven years. Anna had been at her company for nearly fifteen years. While she liked her employer, she wasn't feeling a sense of meaning or purpose in her career anymore. She also felt frustrated and annoyed that she had allowed so much time to go by without making a change. When we explored her needs, she realized she valued security and safety, both of which she had at her job. Her department alone had over ten people who had been there for fifteen-plus years. Plus, her company provided her with a generous compensation package. It was hard to leave such a secure job.

If you are hard on yourself about staying in a position or with an employer for too long, what has been keeping you there?

Be kind to yourself. All your needs are important; you are choosing the ones that are priorities.

3. What needs are keeping you stuck?

If you need help identifying your needs, please reference page 241.

_____

_____

_____

IF YOU'RE STUCK, WHAT NEEDS WILL DRIVE YOU INSTEAD?

If you've been stuck, it's helpful to identify a need or value that will help you make a change. There must be a need or value that is more compelling than the ones that are keeping you there.

Anna ended up pivoting from her job as a compliance manager at an aerospace employer to a data analyst job at a cancer research institution. She had lost both of her parents to cancer and wanted to make an impact in a way that did not require her to go back to school. Anna's needs for meaning and purpose drove her more than her need for security and safety. This gave her the courage to leave her secure job. Luckily, Anna found her needs for security and safety were met at her new job, too.

4. What needs will drive you instead of the needs that are keeping you stuck?

If you need help identifying your needs, please reference page 241.

_____

_____

_____

THE IMPACT YOU LIKE TO MAKE THROUGH YOUR WORK IS CONNECTED TO YOUR VALUES

If you look at your happy career memory (page 45, Freeing Mindset), what was the outcome or the results of your work? Did you complete a project and feel pride in your work, make someone feel better, receive acknowledgment for all you did, create something that gave you a sense of accomplishment, or something else?

The impact you like to make on others or through your work mirrors your values.

I value connection, belonging, creativity and novelty. I feel satisfied when I can create novel experiences to help others find work where they feel belonging and connection.

Diana values mentorship, security, gratitude, and contribution. Diana feels the most satisfied when she can mentor others to build financial security and feel that their needs are provided for.

As much as it's important to use your Driving Talents in your work, the outcome you produce from using them needs to bring you fulfillment and satisfaction as well.

When you look at your values, what impact or contribution do you want to make through your work?

5. What impact or contribution do you want to make through your work? Add it to your True North Guide (page 18).

_____

_____

_____

LIVE IN ALIGNMENT WITH YOUR NEEDS AND VALUES.

Having a career that is aligned with your needs and values will bring more fulfillment.

When your work and employer align with your values, you minimize the likelihood that you'll be put in situations that make you feel uncomfortable. You will also be less likely to burn out or lose interest in your work.

You may need to shift your roles and responsibilities, the impact you make, your industry, your employer, the people you work with, your area of study, or a combination of these elements to meet your needs.

When I started my business, I made a commitment to honor my values of connection, belonging, creativity, and novelty. If I didn't feel a connection with a client, I referred them to another coach. When I facilitate groups, I create a space where everyone feels a sense of belonging. I also follow a schedule that allows time for creativity and trying new things.

Diana pursued a career as a financial counselor working for a company that supported military families. She honors her values of mentorship and security by acting as a mentor and helping military families achieve financial security. She feels a kinship with her coworkers because they share the same mission. Her coworkers show their appreciation to one another, and she feels grateful to be working in a job that is so aligned with her values.

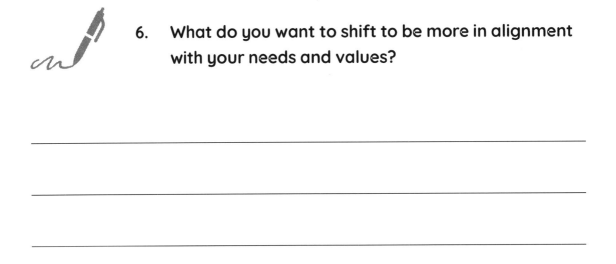

6. What do you want to shift to be more in alignment with your needs and values?

LESSON 5

YOUR DRIVING TALENTS

YOUR DRIVING TALENTS ARE YOUR INNATE ABILITIES THAT GIVE YOU SO MUCH SATISFACTION AND FULFILLMENT, YOU WANT TO GO TO WORK SO YOU CAN USE THEM.

YOU HAVE DONE A LOT OF WORK to identify your Driving Talents in Lessons 1-3. The purpose of this lesson is to narrow them down and clarify how to apply your Driving Talents in your career.

A fulfilling career will capitalize on your Driving Talents. You may have had some jobs that have paid you to use them, or you may have used them regardless of the position. The trick is identifying and pivoting your career to use them fully.

Here are the benefits of working in a career that uses your Driving Talents: 1) as long as the work culture is a good fit, you will thrive in your job; 2) you will hone your skills and further develop your expertise; 3) you will increase your net worth because you are being paid to use the talents by which you are most motivated; 4) you will feel your work is much more meaningful and purposeful.

In the first part of this lesson, you will be looking at the survey responses from your friends, family, and coworkers. Getting an outside perspective can help you understand how your Driving Talents show up in the world. It can also help you decide how you want to use them moving forward.

Ariel, a 28-year-old freelance writer, felt stuck and unsure if she wanted to continue copywriting. She worked for herself for five years and debated if she wanted to get a marketing job or go back to school to become a therapist. Before she did the survey, Ariel knew that one of her Driving Talents was creating and didn't know if she had a second Driving Talent.

As a child, Ariel loved to read fiction books, and her positive memories involved creating things with others, but she hadn't been able to see how those two pieces of the puzzle fit together. She asked me, "How does reading as a child indicate my Driving Talent?" I told her that the answer would reveal itself as we continued through the process.

When Ariel reached the Inner Compass Process survey section, she asked her friend Brenda the first survey question about her top talents. Brenda's response was, "You're empathetic. You are very good at seeing where people are and helping them move forward." When she asked Brenda what she thought she should do for a living, Brenda responded, "I could see you as a therapist."

After reflecting on Brenda's response, Ariel realized that her second Driving Talent was empathizing. She understood that she loved reading because she could live a character's experience and care about their story. After completing the Inner Compass Process, Ariel decided to go back to graduate school and pursue a master's of mental health counseling with a specialization in art therapy, which would allow her to combine her Driving Talents of creating and empathizing.

Like Ariel, I hope you gain a lot of clarity and have some aha moments when reading your survey responses.

How to Approach the Surveys You Received

If you haven't received responses to your survey or the answers you received don't go into enough depth, it can be enlightening to call people up and have conversations instead.

When you look at your feedback, lead with curiosity. If you like what you hear, use it. If you don't like what you hear, let it go.

PRO TIP

My clients find it very helpful to have a trusted friend or career coach to assist with going over the surveys. Someone else might notice or pay attention to different aspects of the surveys than you would. Also, you may take your natural gifts for granted. You might not even realize that your Driving Talents are unique to you.

As you do this, take notes or have your friend take notes for you so you can reflect on them when you are done.

This exercise aims to use the feedback to clarify your Driving Talents and how you might use them in your career.

Are you ready? Let's dive in!

The Process for Looking at Your Survey Results

Here is a walk-through of each step you'll go through to deepen your self-knowledge using the survey results.

You might decide to summarize the feedback from others and look for trends and patterns. You might find that people say similar things about your Driving Talents or provide similar examples of when you were most fulfilled in your work. Or, like Ariel, one person's feedback may nail it and you might use it to help you clarify your Driving Talents moving forward.

A word of caution: If you sent this survey to coworkers who see you working in your Binding Mindset or in a job that doesn't capitalize on your Driving Talents, they might list adjectives that don't fully describe how you want to be in the world or skills that burn you out. Please read these responses with this in mind.

For each question, I've provided examples from Josh, the thirty-eight-year-old mortgage broker mentioned in Lesson 1. Josh had been considering a career change for several years because he had been in the mortgage industry for twelve years and felt that something was missing. During our complimentary consultation, he shared that he loved his work but felt he wasn't making an impact on the world.

Josh found the lesson on Driving Talents insightful and one of the most compelling reasons he decided to stay in his career. The surveys provided tremendous insight and validation that he was making a difference for his supervisees and coworkers in his career.

In addition, I've shared examples from Matthew, the twenty-eight-year-old legal assistant turned network engineer from Lesson 3. Matthew worked as a legal assistant even though it didn't capitalize on his Driving Talents because his father wanted him to become a lawyer. When Matthew received his survey responses, he was able to see how he used his Driving Talents at work despite them not being the focus of his job.

As you read this lesson to clarify your Driving Talents, you'll be reading through Josh and Matthew's examples.

YOUR DRIVING TALENTS

The first question of the survey asks respondents to share one or two of your top talents. What did people say were your top talents?

When I surveyed friends, family, and clients, they shared my top talents: connecting, creating, and coaching. My friends described me as a connector and creator. Many of them described events, parties, retreats I had planned. When I surveyed clients, they defined me as a coach who helped them establish deeper self-awareness and direction. This reinforced what I already knew about my Driving Talents of connecting and creating, although I decided not to use the word "coaching" as my Driving Talent, because coaching does not truly motivate me.

I defined my Driving Talents as:
- Connecting- I help individuals connect with themselves and one another.
- Creating- I like to build original and novel things.

Josh received feedback from several colleagues, clients, friends, and family members. His colleagues and close friends described him as a leader, advisor, and competent communicator. Josh considered himself a leader and advisor, but the idea of being a competent communicator was new for him. When thinking about his Driving Talents, he decided that skillful communication was a subset of his leadership abilities.

Josh defined his Driving Talents as:
- Leading- I like to help others move toward a common goal.
- Advising- I like to help others make sound decisions.

Matthew's friends called him a computer whiz, engineer of all trades, and tech-savvy. His supervisor described him as good with technology. Matthew realized that despite it not being part of his job description, he spent a lot of time at work solving technology issues for his coworkers. While Matthew's feedback was technology-specific, Matthew decided to continue using the word "strategizing" as his Driving Talent because it encompassed his ability to solve problems, especially with technology.

Mathew defined his Driving Talent as:
- Strategizing- I like to solve problems, especially with technology.

THE INNER COMPASS PROCESS

1. List the top talents people described.

_____

_____

_____

2. Did this reinforce what you already know? Do you see similar themes that can be combined into an overarching Driving Talent?

_____

_____

_____

Now that you've identified your Driving Talents in how you like to play, in your positive memories, in your negative memories, and in others' feedback about you, it's time to add them to your True North Guide.

3. **What are your one or two Driving Talents? What is your simple definition of them? Add them to your True North Guide (page 18).**

Please reference pages 33 (Play Your Way to Clarity), 51 (Freeing Mindset), and 65 (Binding Mindset) to see what you wrote down.

_____

_____

_____

ADJECTIVES USED TO DESCRIBE YOU

The second question asked respondents to list adjectives used to describe you to get to the heart of your personality —your personality orients you to be good at your Driving Talents. Let's say your Driving Talent is thinking, your personality might be analytical, observant, and intuitive. If your Driving Talent is mediating, your personality might be calm, attentive, reflective and easy going.

When you see how people describe you, it helps you understand how your intrinsic personality supports your Driving Talents. It can be challenging to recognize that you excel at something, but when you see how your respondents view you, it can help you take ownership of your abilities.

My survey respondents described me as friendly, intelligent, adventurous, explorative, intuitive, direct, engaging, deep, creative, and hard-working. These traits were similar to how I described myself as reflective, friendly, curious, adventurous, and resourceful. I was excited to receive the feedback that others recognized my hard work. My friendly, intuitive, engaging, deep, and creative personality directly contributes to my Driving Talents of creating and connecting.

Josh's survey respondents described him as knowledgeable, informative, friendly, charming, funny, influential, personable, and commanding. These personality traits were similar to how he described himself as social, happy-go-lucky, playful, and easygoing. While he thought he had an easygoing personality, he felt that it was interesting that others perceived him as influential and commanding. It helped him take ownership of his Driving Talent of leading.

Matthew's survey respondents listed him as trustworthy, determined, compassionate, problem-solving, analyzing, and adaptable. He realized that his ability to strategize was supported by his traits of problem-solving, analyzing, and adaptability. Even though his qualities of trustworthiness, determination, and compassion weren't directly tied to his Driving Talent of strategizing, they were still important, because he was known for supporting others.

4. List the adjectives used to describe you. How do they connect to your Driving Talents?

_____

_____

_____

In addition to helping you take ownership of your Driving Talents, the adjectives used to describe you might also inspire you to bring forth the best parts of your personality more often. On the other hand, they may reveal a trait that you currently don't express that you want to project.

When I read the list of adjectives people said about me, I realized that I wanted to express my friendliness more often. Sometimes I find myself closed off from others, and to overcome my Binding Mindset, I intentionally step into my quality of friendliness. Like the wisdom of opposites I shared about overcoming your Binding Mindset in Lesson 3, expressing a positive trait can help you overcome your bind.

I had a client who wanted to express more patience in her work. Her Driving Talent was being able to execute and get things done, but in her focus on achievement, she often found herself losing patience. When she saw the list of adjectives from her respondents, she wasn't surprised that patience wasn't mentioned. She decided to make a practice of patience and to be more patient with herself and others.

5. Are there any adjectives listed that surprised you? Were there any you want to express more often? Is there a trait that people didn't list that you want to embody more?

___

___

___

EXAMPLES OF WHEN YOU USED YOUR DRIVING TALENTS

The third question of the survey asks respondents to share examples of when you used your top gifts or talents. The goal of this question is to provide some insights as to how you solve problems personally and professionally.

My friend shared an example of when I organized a mini-retreat over the winter break for friends to gather and present self-reflective workshops. My partner shared an example of a recent presentation I had given for a professional association. Both of these examples link my two Driving Talents of creating and connecting.

Before the recent feedback, I had mostly been doing individual coaching in my practice. It was interesting to see my loved ones project how much I enjoyed giving presentations and sharing information. It made me realize that pivoting my business to focus on public speaking, presentations, and online courses would help me use my Driving Talent of creating more often.

Josh's mother wrote, "While I have not worked with you, when you were a teen, your friends looked up to you as the captain of the football team. You also shined in your volunteer work at church." Josh's supervisee wrote, "You are one of the best mentors I've ever had. Most bosses do not give you the time of day and just want you to get the job done. I feel like I can go to you with questions. Not only do you help me get my job done, but I've also gotten better at my job with your guidance." He saw how his Driving Talent of leading had been with him

Josh did not realize how much his supervisees valued his advising and supervision. This feedback helped him realize how much of an impact he made on others through his work.

Josh also thought it was interesting that his mother had seen his leadership abilities as a teen. While his mother has never worked with him professionally, she noticed his Driving Talents from a young age. Josh's mother also helped him realize how much he missed volunteering in his free time.

Matthew's mom and dad wrote that he set up computer networks around the house. His supervisor noted that he fixed the office's computer systems and was often the go-to for technological problems, even though that wasn't his job. Matthew knew that working with technology was what he wanted to do, and when he saw his survey responses, it reinforced his insights.

6. **What are some examples of when you used your Driving Talents?**

_____

_____

_____

What insights can you glean from these examples? This is purposefully a very open-ended question, and there is no right or wrong way to answer it.

7. **What insights can you glean from these examples?**

_____

_____

_____

WHEN HAVE YOU NOTICED ME MOST FULFILLED IN MY WORK? WHAT WAS I DOING?

The survey's fourth question asks respondents to share insights about when you were most fulfilled in your work. The purpose of this question is to help you see some more examples of when others see you fulfilled. It also provides insights as to how you might want to pivot your work or roles and responsibilities.

I most recently surveyed my partner to get an idea of what he perceives about my Driving Talents. When I asked him when I seemed the most fulfilled by my work, he shared it was when he saw me through my office window, getting excited to explain concepts to clients. It helped me realize how much I love sharing my ideas and how excited I am to share them on a bigger platform. My creativity has been wanting to manifest in the expression of my ideas.

Josh's colleagues said he was at his best when he was training new mortgage officers and employees. They said he had a strong ability to teach others how to master their jobs and was an influential team leader. He realized that his position already allowed him to use his Driving Talents in his work.

Matthew's coworker shared that he seemed the most fulfilled when he solved a computer networking issue at work that no one else could fix. He got a lot of satisfaction from figuring out how the computers worked together and seeing how to solve technology problems. This insight furthered his self-awareness and solidified his decision to move into a position where he could use more of his Driving Talent for strategizing.

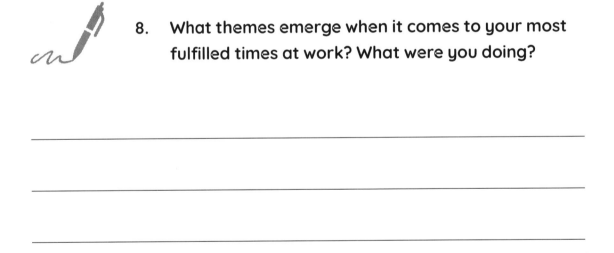

8. What themes emerge when it comes to your most fulfilled times at work? What were you doing?

___

___

___

While Josh, Michael, and I felt our feedback was accurate, if the feedback you received was overall inaccurate, you might want to ask yourself several follow up questions such as: What do you want to project into the world instead? What are some other moments in your life that you've been fulfilled? What do you wish others would say about you instead?

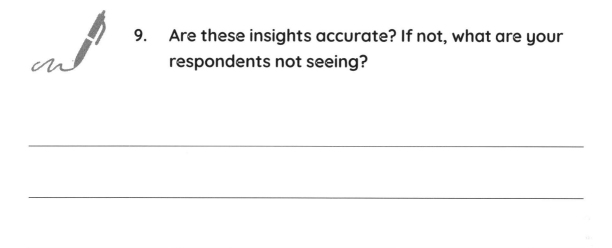

9. Are these insights accurate? If not, what are your respondents not seeing?

___

___

___

WHEN HAVE YOU NOTICED ME MOST DISCONTENT IN MY WORK? WHAT WERE THE CIRCUMSTANCES?

The fifth question of the survey asked respondents when they have noticed you most discontent in your work? What were the circumstances? This question reveals experiences when others see you are not using your Driving Talents.

People I surveyed noted that I appeared burned out of coaching the same programs repeatedly. This revealed the times when I wasn't using my Driving Talent of creating.

Josh's colleagues said that he became frustrated with paperwork and some of the repetitive aspects of project management. While Josh agreed with their feedback, he shared that his dislike for redundancy was not enough to deter him from doing his job.

Matthew's colleague wrote that he didn't see him becoming a lawyer, because he didn't think Matthew enjoyed his job. Matthew's partner also shared concerns about Matthew becoming a lawyer and commented that he didn't seem happy in his career in general.

Almost every job will require you to have some responsibilities that don't use your Driving Talents. Josh's job allowed him to use his Driving Talents of leading most of the time. The paperwork was a minor part of his job that he could live with. However, Matthew's job as a legal assistant only allowed him to use his Driving Talents of strategizing when there happened to be a computer issue. Most of his work required him to do things that weren't within the scope of his Driving Talents. In his case, it made sense to seek a new career where he could use his Driving Talents as a primary function of his position.

10. **What themes emerge when it comes to your most discontent times at work? What were you doing?**

_____

_____

_____

11. **Are these insights accurate? If not, what are your respondents not seeing?**

_____

_____

_____

IS THERE A WAY THAT YOUR DRIVING TALENTS WANT TO EVOLVE?

While feedback is super helpful, it does not capture all of you and how your Driving Talents want to manifest in the world.

Sometimes, the feedback you receive from survey respondents only captures what you've done previously, not where you want to go.

I want to evolve my Driving Talent of creating by producing new programs and not doing the same coaching program repeatedly. I want to further my Driving Talent of connecting by sharing my work with larger audiences.

Josh wanted to use his Driving Talents of leading and advising to better other people's lives. He decided that he was content enough to want to stay in his position and joined the Rotary Club to use his Driving Talent of leading to improve others' lives outside of work.

Matthew decided he wanted to use his Driving Talent of strategizing in the space that interested him the most: technology. He enrolled in certification courses to become a network engineer and updated his skillset. His current position as a junior networking engineer at a national security company allows him to use his Driving Talent of strategizing as a primary part of his job.

When you think about your Driving Talents, is there a way you'd like to use them that you haven't used them before?

12. Is there a way that your Driving Talents want to evolve?

_____

_____

_____

LESSON 6

CONNECT THE DOTS: WHY YOU DO WHAT YOU DO

FROM WHAT I'VE EXPERIENCED PERSONALLY and observed with my clients, using your Driving Talents is the most direct way to feel purpose in your life. In this section, you will revisit parts of the Inner Compass Process and see how your Driving Talents are woven through every aspect of your story.

This lesson is one of my favorite parts of the Inner Compass Process, because clients get to see how their Driving Talents relate to what motivates them deeply. These connections drive home the importance and purpose behind your Driving Talents, and they show why they are at the core of who you are, the most authentic expression of you.

As you go through this lesson, jot down your ideas. It will help you find even more purpose and meaning in your Driving Talents.

HOW YOU LIKE TO PLAY

How did you like to play as a child? How do you like to play now? Your childhood play was likely the first time your Driving Talents showed up in your life, and how you play now has kernels of your Driving Talents in it as well.

When I was a child, I loved being outdoors and adventurous. I also liked completing art projects and attending art classes. As I transitioned into middle and high school, I enjoyed creating programs and events for my youth group. As an adult, my play looks similar, and I enjoy using my Driving Talents of creating and connecting.

Michael, the twenty-six-year-old sales representative from the first lesson, had a Driving Talent for building. He loved playing with LEGO and Erector sets as a kid and enjoys building furniture as an adult. He created a furniture building business so that he could be paid to do what he loves.

Play is what you choose to do when you are free to do anything. You choose these activities because they are innate to you and make you happy. Using your Driving Talents at work means that, in a sense, you are being paid to play.

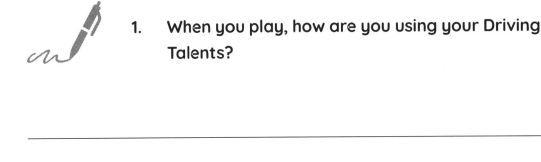

1. When you play, how are you using your Driving Talents?

_____

_____

_____

YOUR POSITIVE OR HAPPY MEMORY FROM CHILDHOOD

Now let's look at your positive memory from childhood. How did you feel when this event happened? It is probably similar to the feelings you experience when living out your Driving Talents.

When I was a little kid hiking with my family in Dickerson, Maryland, I felt warm and connected. When I'm using my Driving Talents of creating and connecting, I experience similar feelings.

When Mae, the content director, was using her gift of creating, she felt just as she did when she was a child in her happy memory of creating pipe-cleaner creatures and going on biking adventures—adventurous and engrossed.

2. **When you live out your Driving Talents, what feelings do they evoke?**

Please reference page 43 to review your feelings.

_____

_____

_____

YOUR POSITIVE OR HAPPY MEMORY FROM YOUR CAREER

Now let's journey to your positive or happy memory from your career. What were you doing? How did you do it? What problem were you solving? If you look closely, you'll probably see that you were using your Driving Talents.

My positive memory in my career was when I organized a yoga class for my high school students. I was using my Driving Talents of creating and connecting in that memory.

Mae's positive memory in her career was working on a campaign that brought attention to a medical device that she was representing. She shared that she was fully using her Driving Talent of creating in this memory.

 3. Were you using your Driving Talents during your positive memory of your career? If not, what are the commonalities of your positive memory and your Driving Talents?

Please reference page 45 to review your positive memory from your career.

_____

_____

_____

YOUR VALUES

What values did you identify as being most important to you in the workplace? How did you define them? **These values show the belief system that allows you to live out your Driving Talents.**

My values are connection, belonging, creativity, and novelty.

I work part-time at a high school as a college advisor. One of the many reasons I work there is because the culture shares my values for connection and belonging. The school provides many opportunities for the community to connect, such as study groups, festivals, and community events. Since I feel that sense of connection and belonging, I can be myself and use my Driving Talents of creating and connecting in my college counseling work.

I spend one to two hours meditating every day because I value creativity in my business, and meditating helps my creative flow. I manifest my Driving Talents of creating in my business by writing books, building courses, and presenting workshops to various organizations.

Diana, the fifty-three-year-old financial counselor for a military contractor from Lesson 2, values security, gratitude, and contribution. Her Driving Talent is advising and mentoring others. In advising her clients, she embodies all of her values. She is able to live out her vision of giving others financial security, and she feels grateful she is able to contribute to the world in a meaningful way.

4. **What is the connection between your values and your Driving Talents?**

Please reference page 18 to review your values.

_____

_____

_____

LESSON 7

THE BEST USE OF YOUR TIME AND SKILLS

YOU'VE WORKED SO HARD to do the more in-depth work to understand Freeing Mindset, Binding Mindset, core values, Driving Talents, and why you do what you do. To love your career, you have to utilize these so that you can spend your day using your skills in ways that are fulfilling to you.

Roles and responsibilities are the tasks or duties of a position. **A skill is an ability to perform a task.** It's something we learn and develop, such as researching, computing, project management, and computer programming. Your skills help you reinforce your Driving Talents, and your Driving Talents help you develop your skills.

The problem is that people get sucked into careers where they use their talents and skills to meet the needs of an employer to the detriment of their own fulfillment. This often happens to job seekers who only look at jobs where they feel qualified but that don't necessarily use their Driving Talents. This also happens to individuals that "fall into a career" and stop taking active measures to correct their course and meet their needs.

A big part of the Inner Compass Process is owning how you want to spend your day and finding jobs that align with it so that you use your time, talents, and skills in ways that are fulfilling to you. Your needs are met, and the employer's needs are met, so it's a win-win situation.

During this lesson, you will identify the best use of time and skills so that you can get a clear picture of a fulfilling workday.

First, you will look back on previous jobs to see which skills, roles, and responsibilities you liked and disliked. Then you will complete a skills assessment to determine how proficient you are at specific skills and how much you want to do them. You will dive deep into three types of skills: those you are great at and want to do a lot (your On Fire Skills), those that you want to improve and use more (your Heating Up Skills), and those that burn you out (your Burnout Skills). Finally, you will assign a percentage to each On Fire and Heating Up Skill to visualize how much time you want to devote to each skill during a workday.

I've provided examples from Gabriel, a thirty-eight-year-old senior business analyst for a large consulting firm, throughout this lesson.

Gabriel pursued career coaching because he felt that his work supporting large corporations with their go-to-market strategy lacked meaning, and while he was good at his job, he felt dissatisfied. He wanted help finding meaningful work like the work he did when he served in the Peace Corps in his twenties. In addition, he wanted a position that provided him the financial security to support a future family.

Gabriel discovered that teaching was his Driving Talent during the process. He defined teaching as the giving and receiving of knowledge. While his work as a senior analyst allowed him to share knowledge with his clients, it didn't meet his need to contribute and serve a population that did not have the resources. He also felt bored with his roles and responsibilities and wanted a change.

After completing the Inner Compass Process, Gabriel started working for a local chamber of commerce as an administrator and small-business consultant. His job included teaching business strategy to small locally owned businesses that could benefit from low-cost resources. Gabriel found a position that was more aligned with his values, Driving Talents, and skills.

A BLAST TO YOUR PAST

One of the best ways to pinpoint what you want to do next in your career is to reflect on previous jobs and think about what you liked and didn't like.

Evaluating Roles and Responsibilities: Your Likes and Dislikes

Using your résumé and past job descriptions, copy and paste your job titles and the corresponding skills, roles, and responsibilities that you liked and didn't like into the spaces below.

You can also share your likes and dislikes from volunteering, side hustles, gigs, freelance work, helping a friend or loved one, a creative project that you did at home, or something to that nature.

As you go through this section, take notes on patterns in both your likes and dislikes. These patterns will help you move toward jobs that use the skills, roles, and responsibilities you liked and away from jobs where you would be doing things you disliked.

I always enjoyed positions that involved developing curriculum or programming. My least favorite positions included having to complete a lot of paperwork or having a lot of downtime.

Gabriel enjoyed producing efficiencies and implementing projects. He also liked using data to help others make decisions, but he disliked getting stuck in the weeds of data analysis, computing, and reporting.

1. **Think back to each job you've had. Write your title and what you liked and didn't like about it.**

Use your résumé and paste your previous job descriptions to guide you.

JOB TITLE	YOUR LIKES	YOUR DISLIKES

2. **Did you notice any patterns in your likes? Add them to your True North Guide (page 19).**

_____

_____

_____

3. **Did you notice any patterns in your dislikes? Add them to your True North Guide (page 19).**

_____

_____

_____

NOW

Now that you've reflected on what you liked and disliked in past jobs, it's time to analyze your skills.[5] In this section, you will evaluate your skills based on how much you enjoy them and how good you are at doing them. This is also known as the best use of your time and skills.

Assessing Your Skills

The three most important skill categories are On Fire, Burnout, and Heating Up Skills. At the end of the assessment, you will be going back and looking at these three categories in greater depth.

- **On Fire Skills** are those you're great at *and* want to do every day. These are the skills you want to be using most of the time in your job.
- **Heating Up Skills** are those you enjoy and want to improve. Even though you aren't as proficient at these skills, you want to bring them into your career more daily.
- **Burnout Skills** are those you're good or even great at but that burn you out. You use these skills heavily in your current job, but you don't want to do them every day in your next one.

The other two categories are Lukewarm and Cold Skills.

- **Lukewarm Skills** are those you are good at and want to use occasionally. You're not as excited about them as On Fire Skills, but you still want to do them some of the time.
- **Cold Skills** are those that you're not great at, and you don't want to do. You may have never used these skills at any job, and you don't want to use them at a job in the future.

For each section below, mark the box that best fits how you feel about that skill. If you would like to add any skills to each section, there are spaces for you to do so.

I've included definitions underneath each skill. You may read them if you like, or you can simply check the box. When you have finished taking the assessment, you'll get a chance to redefine the most important skills, so don't worry if my definitions aren't quite the same as yours.

You will also have the opportunity to add additional skills that haven't been listed.

Please feel free to use the feedback survey from friends, family, and coworkers to add other skills that might not have been listed.

ANALYTICAL SKILLS

You can add additional skills, such as auditing, data analysis (business, cost, credit, policy, process, qualitative, quantitative, SWOT), classifying, calculating, categorizing, inductive reasoning, deductive reasoning, record keeping, predictive modeling, physical data modeling, strategic planning, and troubleshooting.

You can also add areas of expertise, such as biology, engineering, physics, and nanotechnology.

SKILL	ON FIRE I'm great at it and want to do it every day.	HEATING UP I enjoy it and want to improve.	BURNOUT I'm good at it, but it burns me out.	LUKEWARM I'm good at it and want to do it sometimes.	COLD I'm not that great at it/ I don't want to do it.
RESEARCH To investigate and study materials and sources in order to establish facts and reach new conclusions					
ANALYZE To study and determine the relationship of ideas, data, or problems					
DATA MANAGEMENT AND COMPUTATION To collect data and calculate it					
BUDGET To manage numbers and finances					

OTHER SKILL:					
OTHER SKILL:					
OTHER SKILL:					

MANAGEMENT SKILLS

You can add additional skills, such as delegation, hiring, motivating, and team building.

SKILL	ON FIRE I'm great at it and want to do it every day.	HEATING UP I enjoy it and want to improve.	BURNOUT I'm good at it, but it burns me out.	LUKEWARM I'm good at it and want to do it sometimes.	COLD I'm not that great at it/ I don't want to do it.
LEAD To motivate others to get on board with your ideas and to work toward a greater vision					
MANAGE PEOPLE To support employees to work toward business goals					
MANAGE PROJECTS To set goals, timelines, and task management to work toward the completion of a project					

The Best Use of Your Time and Skills

ENVISION To come up with ideas or big-picture goals for the employer to follow					
MAKE DECISIONS To weigh out options and make decisions without supervision or guidance					
INITIATE To take action with little supervision or guidance					
PROCESS IMPROVEMENT To improve upon an idea, concept, or process					
OTHER SKILL:					
OTHER SKILL:					
OTHER SKILL:					

INTERPERSONAL SKILLS

You can add additional skills, such as advising, mentoring, career/nutritional/health coaching, and networking.

SKILL	ON FIRE I'm great at it and want to do it every day.	HEATING UP I enjoy it and want to improve.	BURNOUT I'm good at it, but it burns me out.	LUKEWARM I'm good at it and want to do it sometimes.	COLD I'm not that great at it/ I DON'T WANT TO DO IT.
TEACH To instruct or train others to understand materials and content					
COACH To help a person improve performance and accomplish goals					
COUNSEL To support others through personal, social, or psychological problems					
CONSULT To evaluate a client's needs and then provide expertise, advice, and suggestions					
FACILITATE GROUPS To guide groups through discussion and exercises					

The Best Use of Your Time and Skills

RESOLVE CONFLICT To help parties address conflict and reach a mutual agreement					
COLLABORATE To work with others to create or strategize					
CUSTOMER SERVICE To work with customers to meet their needs and exceed their expectations					
OTHER SKILL:					
OTHER SKILL:					
OTHER SKILL:					

COMMUNICATION SKILLS

You can add additional skills, such as developing trust, establishing rapport, empathy/emotional intelligence, nonverbal communication, and providing feedback.

SKILL	ON FIRE I'm great at it and want to do it every day.	HEATING UP I enjoy it and want to improve.	BURNOUT I'm good at it, but it burns me out.	LUKEWARM I'm good at it and want to do it sometimes.	COLD I'm not that great at it/ I don't want to do it.
WRITE To write in order to share a concept or idea					
PRESENT To speak in front of groups in order to present ideas					
SELL To influence someone to purchase products or services					
NEGOTIATE To come up with an agreement that involves a transference of ownership					
CONVERSE To listen and speak to others one-on-one or in a small group					
PERSUADE To convince others to follow a course of action					
OTHER SKILL:					

OTHER SKILL:					
OTHER SKILL:					

CREATIVE SKILLS

SKILL	ON FIRE I'm great at it and want to do it every day.	HEATING UP I enjoy it and want to improve.	BURNOUT I'm good at it, but it burns me out.	LUKEWARM I'm good at it and want to do it sometimes.	COLD I'm not that great at it/ I don't want to do it.
DESIGN To create a project, program, or product					
CREATE IMAGES To photograph, do graphic design, paint, draw, etc.					
DRAFT To sketch and draw images to relay a concept					
PERFORM To act, sing, dance, or play music					
IDEATION To come up with concepts or ideas					
MAKE CONNECTIONS To connect disparate ideas or concepts					

SKILL					
WRITE CREATIVELY OR COMPOSE To write stories, poems, songs, etc.					
COOK To create recipes and prepare food					
OTHER SKILL:					
OTHER SKILL:					
OTHER SKILL:					

COMPUTER SKILLS

You can add additional skills, such as AI, Point of Sale systems, and video game development.

SKILL	ON FIRE I'm great at it and want to do it every day.	HEATING UP I enjoy it and want to improve.	BURNOUT I'm good at it, but it burns me out.	LUKEWARM I'm good at it and want to do it sometimes.	COLD I'm not that great at it/ I don't want to do it.
MICROSOFT OFFICE AND G SUITE					
PRESENTATION SOFTWARE PowerPoint, Keynote, etc.					
SPREADSHEETS Excel, Google Spreadsheets, etc.					

The Best Use of Your Time and Skills

ACCOUNTING SOFTWARE QuickBooks, FreshBooks, Xero, etc.					
SOCIAL MEDIA Twitter, Facebook, Instagram, etc.					
DATA VISUALIZATION Tableau, Datawrapper, etc.					
COMPUTER PROGRAMMING C++, HTML, Java, Python, etc.					
DIGITAL MARKETING CMS, CSS, SEO, KPI, etc.					
GRAPHIC DESIGN Adobe, InDesign, video creation software					
DATABASES HQL, SAS, SPSS					
IT TROUBLESHOOTING tech support, help desk					
CYBER SECURITY virus protection, malware, risk management					
OTHER SKILL:					
OTHER SKILL:					
OTHER SKILL:					

PHYSICAL SKILLS

You can add additional skills, such as general contracting, handcrafts, masonry, landscaping, etc.

SKILL	ON FIRE I'm great at it and want to do it every day.	HEATING UP I enjoy it and want to improve.	BURNOUT I'm good at it, but it burns me out.	LUKEWARM I'm good at it and want to do it sometimes.	COLD I'm not that great at it/ I don't want to do it.
BUILD To build structures using tools, equipment, or machines					
RENOVATE To bring something back to its original form					
REMODEL To change the structure of something					
REPAIR To fix something that is broken					
INSPECT To evaluate the condition of something					
PHYSICAL ACTIVITY To use your body to perform a task					
USE HANDS To use your hands to perform a task					
OTHER SKILL:					

OTHER SKILL:					
OTHER SKILL:					

IDENTIFY THE BEST USE OF YOUR TIME AND SKILLS

In this section, you will identify which of your On Fire and Heating Up Skills you want to do regularly at work.

After you choose your skills, you will write your own definition of what they mean to you. Think back to your past and how you used them in previous roles. Also, think about your future and how you want to use them moving forward.

The reason you will write your own definition of those skills is that often other people's descriptions might not fit what you envision doing with them.

Sometimes career changers ask, "How do I know if I want to use that skill? Maybe I want to use it because it's all I know." If you are asking yourself this question, simply reflect on if you were to use that skill every day in your job, would you be in your Freeing Mindset or Binding Mindset? If your answer is Freeing Mindset, then you know it's a skill you want to use. Keep in mind, you will also analyze how much time you want to spend in each skill so that you have a balance that works for you.

ANALYZE YOUR ON FIRE SKILLS

Your On Fire Skills are those you want to be doing most of the time in your job or career.

Your On Fire Skills are those that support your Driving Talents meet your core values, and support your current needs. If your Driving Talent is communicating, the skills you might want to use in your job could include writing, persuading, and conversing. If your Driving Talent is planning, the skills you might want to use in your position could involve managing projects, initiating, and process improvement.

One of my On Fire Skills is process improvement. The definition above is "To improve upon an idea, concept, or process." I define it as "To take what I have learned in psychology and career coaching workshops and repurpose it for career changers." I spend thirty percent of my time attending workshops and repurposing the content for my clients. My skill of process improvement allows me to live out my Driving Talent for creating and it satisfies my value of novelty because I can create new experiences for myself and others.

Gabriel chose teaching as one of his top skills. His definition was "to share knowledge about how to include technology to more effectively run a business." This definition was more specific from the one above, which is "instruct or train others to understand materials and content." Gabriel's skill of teaching allowed him to use his Driving Talent of teaching (yes, it's okay that a skill and a Driving Talent are the same). It met his value of helping others and supports his current needs for connection and community.

He personalized the skill and was able to understand how it related to his work. In his past, he enjoyed teaching women in the Peace Corps how to run small businesses. Moving forward, he could picture himself working with small businesses and teaching them how to use technology to solve their problems for at least forty percent of his time on a given day.

4. Which On Fire Skills do you want to use in your career? What do the skills mean to you, and how much time do you see yourself doing them? Add them to your True North Guide (page 19).

MY ON FIRE SKILLS	HOW I DEFINE THEM	PERCENTAGE OF TIME

ANALYZE YOUR HEATING UP SKILLS

Now choose the top three Heating Up Skills that you would like to improve and use in your career.

Heating Up Skills are those you enjoy doing, want to improve upon, and want to do more in the future.

Your Heating Up Skills also support your Driving Talents and assist you in evolving yourself and your career. They can be the areas you want to develop and grow, thus helping you manifest your Driving Talents in new and meaningful ways. In addition, they can help you meet your needs as you change and evolve.

I chose presenting as one of my Heating Up Skills. I've started presenting at conferences more recently, and it's something I want to improve on. My definition of it is "to speak at conferences and share more about my process with other coaches." Since I get nervous in front of audiences, I've been taking online courses to improve my presentation skills. I can see myself spending three to four weekends a year presenting at conferences, so I'm giving it ten percent. My Heating Up Skill of presenting helps me live out my Driving Talents of creating and connecting, and it provides opportunities to meet my need for novelty.

Gabriel chose "manage people" as one of his Heating Up Skills. Even though that wasn't one of his primary skills as a business analyst, it was a skill he enjoyed and wanted to do more. His definition of "manage people" is "I love the idea of managing a team of employees."

While Gabriel did not have any formal job titles that included "manager," he managed two to three junior analysts. Gabriel realized that his next role might not be as a supervisor, but he wanted to look for organizations that had job growth or the possibility of managing others. He decided to read some books on business management and leadership skills and possibly enroll in a reputable business leadership course to build his knowledge. Gabriel shared that he would want to spend twenty percent of his time managing others. Gabriel also shared that managing others as a Heating Up Skills allowed him to teach in a new and different way. It would also support his needs for growth and security.

Now it's your turn. What Heating Up Skills do you want to use in your career? What does that skill mean to you, and how do you envision using it in your career?

5. What Heating Up Skills do you want to use in your career? What does that skill mean to you, and how much time do you see yourself doing it? Add them to your True North Guide (page 19).

MY HEATING UP SKILLS	HOW I DEFINE THEM	PERCENTAGE OF TIME

BURNOUT SKILLS

Now choose the top three Burnout Skills that have made you feel burned out in your career.

You may end up choosing a job in which you'll use these skills, but you don't want to do a job that forces you to use them at a percentage that does not serve you.

Your Burnout Skills can consist of skills that are associated with your Driving Talents, but you need to reduce them significantly or remove them entirely because they don't meet your needs. Your Burnout Skills can also be skills that have nothing to do with your Driving Talents, but you've overused them and don't want to do them anymore.

For example, one of my clients was a secretary, and her Driving Talents were organizing and designing. Some of the skills she used in her secretarial career were filing, email management, database management and travel logistics, but she hated using these skills even though they were connected to her Driving Talent of organizing. They didn't meet her needs for inspiration, beauty and self-expression. She knew she wanted to leave them behind in her next position (she ended up changing careers to interior design).

One of my Burnout Skills is coaching, which can be associated with my Driving Talent of connection. I get exhausted if I do more than two hours a day of coaching. When I first started coaching, it met my need for novelty, because it was a new experience for me. Now that I've been coaching for over seven years, it no longer meets that need, which is why it has changed from an On Fire to a Burnout skill.

I also dislike email management, which has nothing to do with my talents for connecting and creating, but it's a necessary part of my business. I get exhausted from managing my inbox, so much so that I hired an organizational specialist to help me set up my inbox and automatically generate emails.

Gabriel chose "manage data" as one of his Burnout Skills. He's very skilled at managing data, and it was one of the primary skills he used as a business analyst to support clients with evaluating decisions. He wrote that managing data involves getting in the weeds of computing and statistical analysis. He loves using data to make decisions, but he wanted to work with an analyst instead of being an analyst. Managing data took him away from his Driving Talent of teaching.

Note: Your Burnout Skills may burn you out because of *how* you're doing them or *how much time* you're doing them rather than *what* you're doing.

6. What Burnout Skills do you want to leave behind or minimize? Add them to your True North Guide (page 20).

_____

_____

_____

WHAT CHANGES DO YOU WANT TO EXPLORE IN YOUR WORK?

Now that you've had some time to evaluate the best use of your time and skills, what changes might you want to explore in your work?

Which roles and responsibilities and skills do you want to leave behind? On the other hand, which roles and responsibilities and skills do you want to step into? If you were to step into them, how would this allow you to live out your Driving Talents in your work?

By reducing my one-on-one coaching hours, I finally had the time and energy to write this book. I also have more time to prepare presentations for organizations and associations.

By Gabriel minimizing his data management, he was able to step into his Driving Talent of teaching and shift to a more meaningful role as a business advisor at the chamber of commerce.

THE INNER COMPASS PROCESS

7. Based on how you want to spend your time and use your skills, what changes might you want to explore in your work?

_____

_____

_____

PART 2

CAREER EXPLORATION

LESSON 8

JUMP IN AND MAKE A CHANGE

AS YOU'VE PROBABLY REALIZED ALREADY, not everyone who reads this book is going to change careers. Some people stay in their position but shift their roles and responsibilities, or the way they approach their work. Others change jobs, employers, or industries.

Keep in mind that you can make incremental changes. It might be easier to change jobs or companies over changing careers and industries. You can always try one thing, change your mind, and try something else.

I've had many clients change their jobs in the short term and eventually change their careers. I've also had clients initially change employers and ultimately change industries after several roles. The point is, you're never stuck.

In this lesson, you will generate a list of jobs, careers, industries, employers, and/or businesses to research. You are not meant to perform extensive research, but to do just enough to give you some ideas. You should not spend more than three hours on this lesson because Lessons 9 and 10 will guide you even further as to *how* you should do the research.

You've done so much work to identify what is working and not working in your current career. Based on your evaluation of all that reflection and analysis, what change would you like to make.

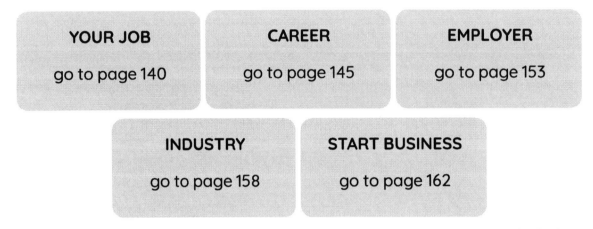

Keep in mind, you can complete multiple sections of this lesson to identify the best change for you.

If you need some further evaluation, take the quiz below.

QUIZ: DO YOU WANT TO CHANGE YOUR JOB, CAREER, EMPLOYER, OR INDUSTRY?

Section 1: Your Job (Roles and Responsibilities)

1. Do your job roles and responsibilities allow for play and enjoyment?
    a. Yes
    b. No
    c. Sometimes

2. Do they allow the best parts of your personality to come through?
   a. Yes
   b. No
   c. Sometimes

3. What do you typically experience when doing your job roles and responsibilities?
   a. My Freeing Mindset
   b. My Binding Mindset
   c. A mix of my Freeing and Binding Mindset

4. Do you feel the roles and responsibilities of your job are in alignment with your values?
   a. Yes
   b. No
   c. Sometimes

5. Do you feel the roles and responsibilities of your job meet your current needs?
   a. Yes
   b. No
   c. Sometimes

6. Do you feel the roles and responsibilities of your job utilize your Driving Talents?
   a. Yes
   b. No
   c. Sometimes

7. Do you feel your job's roles and responsibilities utilize your On Fire and Heating Up Skills while minimizing your Burnout Skills?
   a. Yes
   b. No
   c. Sometimes

I answered mostly: (a)s (b)s or (c)s

___

SECTION 2: YOUR EMPLOYER (WHERE YOU WORK)

1. Does your employer provide opportunities for you to spend your time in a way that feels enjoyable?
   a. Yes
   b. No
   c. I don't know

2. What do you typically experience in your relationships with your supervisors and coworkers?
   a. My Freeing Mindset
   b. My Binding Mindset
   c. A mix of my Freeing and Binding Mindset

3. What do you typically experience when you think about your company?
   a. My Freeing Mindset
   a. My Binding Mindset
   b. A mix of my Freeing and Binding Mindset

4. Do you share similar values with your employer?
   a. Yes
   b. No
   c. Somewhat

5. Does working for your employer meet your current needs?
   a. Yes
   b. No
   c. Somewhat

6. Does your employer pay you to use your Driving Talents?
   a. Yes
   b. No
   c. Sometimes

7. If not, is there a job at your company that can use your Driving Talents?
   a. Yes
   b. No
   c. I don't know

8. Does your employer pay you to use your On Fire and Heating Up Skills?
   a. Yes
   b. No
   c. Sometimes

9. If not, is there a job at your company that can use your On Fire and Heating Up Skills?
   a. Yes
   b. No
   c. I don't know

I answered mostly: (a)s (b)s or (c)s

_____

SECTION 3: YOUR CAREER
(The Various Jobs that You Can Have With Your Current Skill Set, Education, and Training)

You may not know enough about the other positions on your career path to answer the following questions. If you don't know the answers, that's okay. You will learn more about jobs in your career path later in this book.

1. Do you see opportunities to infuse your work with more play from what you know about your career path options?
   a. Yes
   b. No
   c. I don't know

2. When you look at potential options to advance in your career, do you see any jobs that would allow you to experience your Freeing Mindset more often?
   a. Yes
   b. No
   c. I don't know

3. When you look at potential options to advance in your career, do you think the jobs would cause you to experience your Binding Mindset?
   a. Yes
   b. No
   c. I don't know

4. When you think about the options along your career path, can you live out your values?
   a. Yes
   b. No
   c. I don't know

5. When you think about the options along your career path, are there other options that better use your Driving Talents?
   a. Yes
   b. No
   c. I don't know

6. When you think about the options along your career path, are there other options that better use your On Fire and Heating Up skills?
   a. Yes
   b. No
   c. I don't know

I answered mostly: (a)s (b)s or (c)s

SECTION 4: INDUSTRY
(Types of Goods and Services Your Employer Produces)

Only answer these questions if you know you want to stay in your job and your career.

1. Does your industry reflect your interests?
   a. Yes
   b. No
   c. I don't know

2. When you think about impacts of your industry and the work that you do within it, does it align with your values?
   a. Yes
   b. No
   c. Sometimes

I answered mostly: (a)s (b)s or (c)s

---

1. Choose the change you want to make

Mark off your answers for each section in the chart below. Then, based on your answers, proceed to the section that best fits your situation.

	(A)S STAY	(B)S CHANGE	(C)S UNCERTAIN
JOB			
EMPLOYER			
CAREER			
INDUSTRY			

If you have answered mostly (a)s to all of the sections above:

You likely need to make an internal shift to feel fulfilled in your work. Please consider seeking the support of a licensed therapist or coach. I also have a course, *The Inner Compass Leadership Program*, to support you in making these shifts. Please check out my website, innercompasscoach.com, to learn more.

If you answered mostly (b)s about your job, and (a)s OR (c)s about your career:

You may want to change jobs but stay in the same career and/or employer. Go to Lesson 8: Section 1 (page 140). You will look at your career path and decide if any other jobs in your career look like they might be a better fit.

If you answered mostly (b)s about your job and career:

You may want to change careers altogether (which may mean changing companies and industries as well). Go to Lesson 8: Section 2 (page 145). There, you'll be doing a complete career search, looking at career paths of several careers, and creating a list of jobs to research further.

If you answered mostly (a)s about your job and (b)s about your employer:

You may want a similar job but want to change employers. Go to Lesson 8: Section 3 (page 153). You will research employers and generate a list of companies to pursue.

If you answered mostly (a)s about your job and (b)s about your industry:

You may want a similar job but want to change industries. Go to Lesson 8: Section 4 (page 158). You will research industries and generate a list of industries to pursue.

To start your own business:

If you think you may want to start your own business, go to Lesson 8: Section 5 (page 162). There you will come up with business ideas to research further.

SECTION 1: CHANGING JOBS

COME UP WITH A JOB LIST ALONG YOUR CAREER PATH.

This section is for you if you want to stay in your career but change your job roles and responsibilities.

You will identify what job options are available in your current career and then generate a list of jobs to research along your current path.

List generation methods:
- Look at graphics of your career path.
- Get inspiration from the different positions available with your current employer (or former employer).
- Take an assessment to evaluate your transferable skills and find other positions that use those skills.
- Take suggestions from your survey responses.

LOOK AT GRAPHICS OF YOUR CAREER PATH.

One of the easiest ways to see other options in your current career is to look at graphics of your career path. I suggest doing an image search on Google. Type in "[your job or career] [career path, trajectory, or pathways]" and see what comes up.

PayScale also has helpful resources on researching career paths. Check out https://www.payscale.com/career-path-planner.

For example, here is one graphic that comes up when I search for "HR career path."

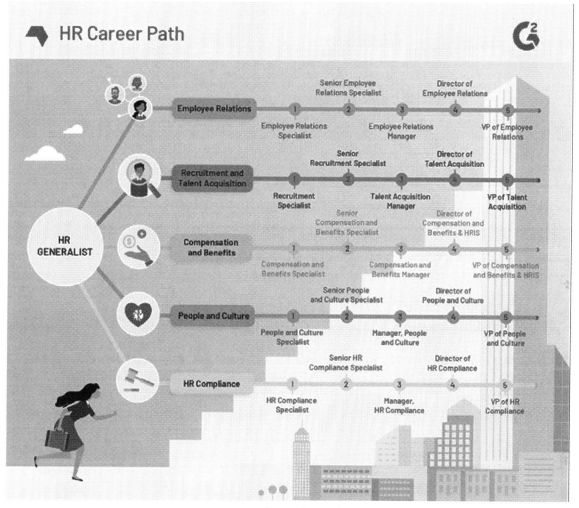

Image Source[6]

By looking at this graphic, you can see how many different types of jobs are available in HR.

1. Write down the job titles within your current career path that spark your interest.

_____

_____

_____

GET INSPIRATION FROM THE DIFFERENT POSITIONS AVAILABLE WITH YOUR CURRENT EMPLOYER (OR FORMER EMPLOYERS).

Think about the different positions available with your current or former employer. Look at the job titles of your coworkers and supervisors. Then go beyond just the positions in your department. Do any of them interest you?

2. Write down the job titles within your place of employment that spark your interest.

_____

_____

_____

TAKE THE MYSKILLS MYFUTURE ASSESSMENT.

Sometimes, it helps to have resources such as assessments to come up with other job options that could be a good fit. The mySkills myFuture assessment will generate a list of possible jobs that use your transferable skills from your current job. Visit https://www.myskillsmyfuture.org/ and enter your current job to see what options come up for you. If any of them interest you, you can click through to find more information.

3. Write down the job titles that spark your interest from mySkills myFuture.

_____

_____

_____

LOOK AT YOUR SURVEY RESPONSES.

Remember the survey I had you give out at the beginning of this process? The last question you asked people was, "What do you think I should be doing for a living and why?" Go back and look at the responses you received from that question, especially from current and former coworkers. Do any of those jobs interest you? Write them down below.

4. What job titles interest you from your survey responses?

_____

_____

_____

YOUR LIST

Look over the jobs you generated in the sections above. Copy and paste four jobs you want to further research below. Remember, you can always come back and add more to your list, but it's easier to start with four and add more if needed.

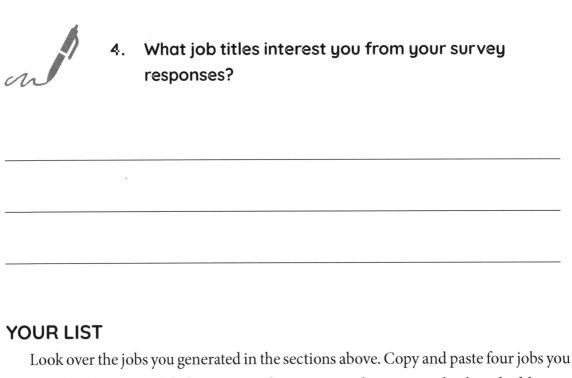

5. Make a list of four jobs you would like to research.

Look over the jobs you generated in the sections above. Copy and paste four jobs you want to further research below. Remember, you can always come back and add more to your list, but it's easier to start with four and add more if needed.

_____

_____

_____

AND WHAT IF I'M NOT FINDING ANYTHING I LIKE?

One of the most frustrating things for job changers is figuring out a job title to target.

One of the reasons you've created your True North Guide is to create a job description for yourself and a guide as to what you want to target.

If you are finding that this initial exercise does not generate a list of titles that you want to research further, you have two options: 1) you can complete another section of your list generation and explore changing careers, employers, or industries; 2) you can jump to the Career Conversations section of this book and talk to people who are in your field to help you identify job titles to target that align with your True North Guide (page 18).

NEXT STEPS

Now that you have your job list, it's time to dig in and do some research. Skip to Lesson 10: Section 1 (page 170) to begin your in-depth research.

SECTION 2: CHANGING CAREERS

COME UP WITH A NEW LIST OF CAREERS TO RESEARCH.

Are you considering leaving your job entirely and changing careers? Awesome. Let's help you generate some ideas of options to research. You're going to come up with a list of jobs to research and gain a better understanding of potential career paths.

Research methods:
- Do some creative search engine research to find career and job ideas.
- Take online assessments.
- Look at career paths.

- Search for nontraditional jobs.
- Take suggestions from your survey responses.

DO SEARCH ENGINE RESEARCH.
What to do:

One of the best ways to generate career ideas is to become a Google whiz. Here's how you're going to do that. First, open your search engine, then use your True North Guide and this section to generate career ideas. Copy and paste these phrases into a search engine and then replace the words in the parenthesis with your own language. Please note, these phrases are not all-encompassing. Rather, they are meant to help you think creatively about what you can search.

Remember, do *not* spend more than three hours on this lesson. If Googling is not generating any ideas, stop what you're doing and skip to the next section.

Careers/jobs that use your likes, On Fire or Heating Up Skills, or interests

- [careers or jobs] for people who love to [insert On Fire or Heating Up Skills, or interests]
  - *EXAMPLES: jobs for people who love creative writing, jobs for people who love to be outside, careers for people who love to talk to people*

- [careers or jobs] that involve [insert On Fire or Heating Up Skills, or interests]
  - *EXAMPLES: jobs that involve teaching, jobs that involve graphic design*

- [careers or jobs] that don't require (insert your dislike)
  - *EXAMPLES: careers that don't require math or science, jobs for introverts, etc.*

Careers/jobs that align with your core values
- [your value] jobs
  - *EXAMPLES: meaningful jobs, creative jobs, jobs for creative people, careers for personal growth, careers that provide job stability*

Careers/jobs that allow you to live out your Driving Talents
- jobs that help people [the impact or contribution you want to make through your work]
- jobs that involve [insert your Driving Talent]

You can add elements, such as salary or education, to your searches as well. Add any of these phrases to the searches above.

Salary
- jobs that pay over X
  - *EXAMPLE: meaningful jobs that pay over 90K*

- highest paying jobs
  - *EXAMPLE: highest-paying jobs for people who love to be outside*

- jobs in [your area or industry] that are the highest paying

Education
- jobs that require an X degree
- jobs that don't require a degree

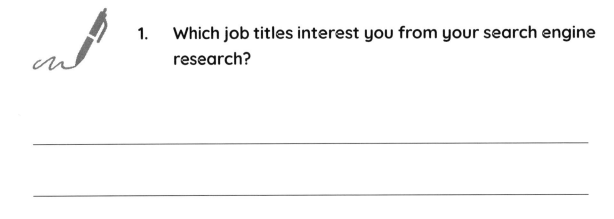 1. Which job titles interest you from your search engine research?

TAKE ONLINE ASSESSMENTS.

You might be wondering, after all this self-assessment, why would you use online assessments? Online assessments can be a great tool to generate new job ideas to research based on your interests, skills, values, strengths, and more. Most readers will find that online assessments will reaffirm what they already know about themselves and might provide some career options that they haven't considered.

However, one downside of career assessments is that the results can be very general, which doesn't help career changers narrow down their options.

Remember, suggestions offered by assessments are just launching points to dig deeper into your career research. Even if a job interests you but is not realistic because it might require too much training and education or does not pay enough, write it down, because you might want to look for careers that have similar qualities but don't require the training and education, or that have higher pay.

Take the initial list of job suggestions, choose the ones that interest you, and then search for their career trajectories or paths. As you continue to research, you will find other options within the career paths that might be a better fit.

Career assessments I recommend:

https://www.careeronestop.org/ExploreCareers/Assessments/self-assessments.aspx

https://www.skillscan.com/

https://www.onetcenter.org/tools.html

https://www.truity.com/

https://www.ncda.org/aws/NCDA/pt/sp/resources (go to the assessments tab)

2. Which job titles interest you from your online assessments?

_____

_____

_____

LOOK AT CAREER PATHS.

You may have found some jobs that look interesting but don't exactly fit what you're looking for. If so, it's helpful to look at career paths to see some of the other options out there. One of the easiest ways to see other options is to look at the graphics of the career path. I suggest doing an image search in Google. Type in "[the job or career] [career path, trajectory, or pathways]" and see what comes up.

PayScale also has helpful resources on researching career paths. Check out https://www.payscale.com/career-path-planner.

3. What job titles interest you from looking at career paths?

_____

_____

_____

LOOK AT NONTRADITIONAL JOBS.

You may know that traditional jobs don't work for you, or you may just be curious about some of the other options out there.

There are nontraditional jobs such as acupuncturist, bed tester, beer drinker, bounty hunter, brewmaster, campground host, casino host, cruise ship staff, crime scene cleanup technician, drone pilot, doula, dominatrix, embalmer, ethical hacker, drone pilot, food stylist, Instagram influencer, musical festival staff, online reviewer, online shopper, panda handler, personal shopper, position-in-line holder, professional bridesmaid, professional cuddler, professional mourner, professional shopper, property caretaker, sex toy tester, sommelier, technical career coach, trip leader, traveling nurse, and voice-over artist.

The key to finding a nontraditional job is to get creative with titles, ideas, and concepts. Search www.jobmonkey.com/ for ideas.

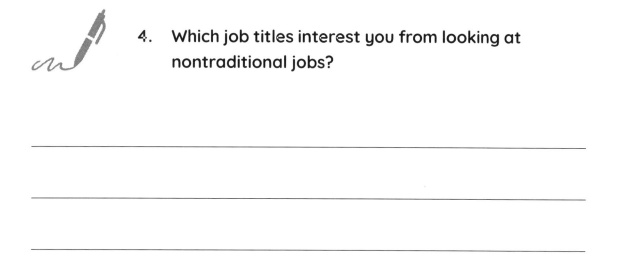

4. Which job titles interest you from looking at nontraditional jobs?

_____

_____

_____

LOOK AT YOUR SURVEY RESPONSES.

Remember the survey I had you give out at the beginning of this process? The last question you asked people was, "What do you think I should do for a living and why?" Go back and look at the responses you received from that question. Do any of those jobs interest you? Write them down below.

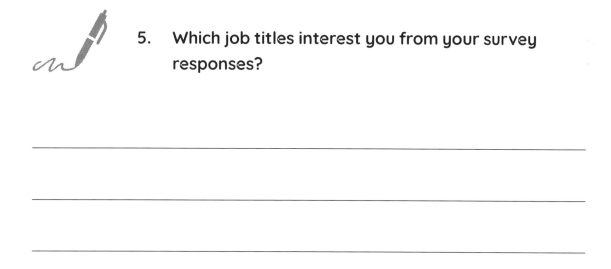

5. Which job titles interest you from your survey responses?

_____

_____

_____

YOUR LIST

Look at all the jobs you've generated from the questions above. Make a list of four jobs that excited you. Remember, you can always come back and add more to your list, but it's easier to start with four and add more if needed.

6. **Make a list of four jobs you would like to research.**

_____

_____

_____

AND WHAT IF I'M NOT FINDING ANYTHING I LIKE?

One of the most frustrating things for job and career changers is figuring out a job title to target.

One of the reasons you've created your True North Guide is to create a job description for yourself and a guide for what you want to target.

If you find that this initial exercise does not generate a list of titles that you want to research further, then jump to the Career Conversations section of this book and use your career conversations to help you with your list generation (page 189).

NEXT STEPS

Now that you have your job list, it's time to dig in and do some research. Skip to Lesson 9: Section 1 (page 170) to begin your in-depth research.

SECTION 3: CHANGING EMPLOYERS

COME UP WITH AN EMPLOYER LIST FOR YOUR RESEARCH

You've decided you want to get a similar job to the one you have now but change your employer. Great! In this section, you will generate a list of employers to research.

Please be aware that you will find most of your opportunities through career conversations (Lesson 10), and that is where you will spend most of your time. However, it does help to have some knowledge about the opportunities out there before you jump in and start talking to people.

List generation methods:
- Write down companies or employers that already interest you.
- Do search engine research.
- Research companies on Glassdoor.
- Look at LinkedIn.
- Search for the economic partnerships or key industries in your state.

LIST EMPLOYERS THAT INTEREST YOU.

You may already have a shortlist of employers that have piqued your interest in the past. It could be because you've heard they're good to their employees, or you may know someone that already works there who likes it. Whatever the case may be, write down your list below. If you don't have a list, skip to the next question

1. **Write down the employers that already interest you.**

_____

_____

_____

DO SEARCH ENGINE RESEARCH.

Another way to find employers is by doing search engine research.

Using your favorite search engine, type in something along the lines of: "best [your industry] companies to work for in [your location]," or "companies that do [list your interest]."

You may need to modify this based on your industry and career. For example, you may already know that you want to work for a startup. In that case, you would type in "best [industry] startups to work for in [your location]."

Or maybe you're looking for more remote work. In that case, you would type in "best [industry] companies that allow employees to work remotely."

Use these ideas as a jumping-off point for your search.

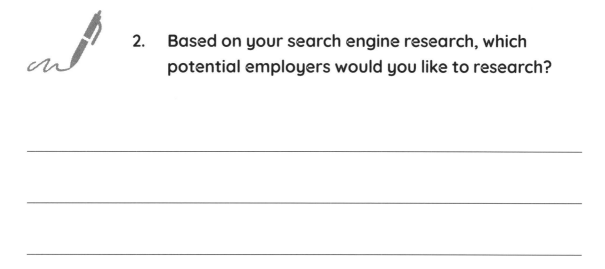

2. Based on your search engine research, which potential employers would you like to research?

___

___

___

RESEARCH COMPANIES ON GLASSDOOR AND PAYSCALE.

Glassdoor and PayScale are excellent sites for learning about employers in your area of interest. You can search for specific companies and read reviews and ratings from current and former employees. If some companies already interest you, you can research them to see if they might be a good fit

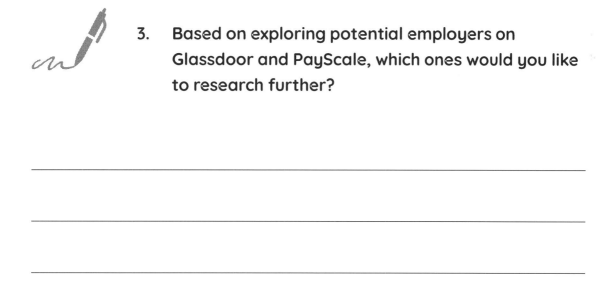

3. Based on exploring potential employers on Glassdoor and PayScale, which ones would you like to research further?

___

___

___

RESEARCH COMPANIES ON LINKEDIN.

Another place to look at companies is LinkedIn. You can look at your connections and see what companies they work for. That will give you an idea of where to start having career conversations in Lesson 10.

4. Based on your research on LinkedIn, which potential employers would you like to research?

_____

_____

_____

SEARCH FOR THE ECONOMIC PARTNERSHIPS OR KEY INDUSTRIES IN YOUR STATE.

Do a Google search for "economic partnerships or key industries in [your state]" for a list of the key employers in your industry. This search will help you see who the largest employers are in your area. Do any of them interest you? Write their names below.

5. **Based on your industry research, what potential employers would you like to research further?**

_____

_____

_____

YOUR LIST

Look at the potential employers you've generated from the questions above. Make a list of four to six employers that excited you. Remember, you can always come back and add more to your list, but it's easier to start with four to six and add more if needed.

6. **Make a list of four to six employers that you would like to research further.**

_____

_____

_____

NEXT STEPS

Now that you have your employer list, it's time to do your research. Skip to Lesson 9: Section 2 (page 178).

SECTION 4: CHANGING INDUSTRIES

COME UP WITH AN INDUSTRY LIST FOR YOUR RESEARCH.

You've decided you want to get a similar job to the one you have now but change your industry. In this section, you will begin to generate a list of industries to research. Then you will get a much better understanding of industries by having career conversations (covered in Lesson 10).

List generation methods:
- Write down industries that already interest you.
- Do search engine research.
- Research industries on the Bureau of Labor Statistics website.
- Search for the economic partnerships or key industries in your state.

LIST INDUSTRIES THAT INTEREST YOU.

You may already have some ideas of industries that interest you. Perhaps you've been following the tech, healthcare, or online retail sectors closely.

1. Write down industries that already interest you.

_____

_____

_____

DO SEARCH ENGINE RESEARCH.

Another way to find industries is by doing search engine research.

Using your favorite search engine, type in something along the lines of "thriving industries during [fill in the blank]."

Or maybe you're looking for more remote work. In that case, you would type in "best [industry] that allow employees to work remotely."

Use these ideas as a jumping-off point for your search.

2. Based on your search engine research, which industries would you like to research further?

_____

_____

_____

RESEARCH INDUSTRIES ON THE U.S. BUREAU OF LABOR STATISTICS WEBSITE.

The Bureau of Labor Statistics website has a list of industries. While it has a robust amount of information, it can be rather cumbersome. More than anything, it can be a launching point to gain ideas. (https://www.bls.gov/iag/)

3. Are there any industries you'd like to explore further after visiting the Bureau of Labor Statistics website?

_____

_____

_____

SEARCH FOR THE KEY INDUSTRIES IN YOUR STATE.

Do a Google search for "key Industries in [your state]" to generate a list of the key industries in your area. Do any of them interest you?

4. Which key industries in your state would you like to research further?

_____

_____

_____

YOUR LIST

Look at the potential industries you've generated from the questions above. Make a list of industries that excited you

5. Based on your research, what industries would you like to research further?

_____

_____

_____

NEXT STEPS

Now that you have your industry list, it's time to do your research. Skip to Lesson 9: Section 3 (page 182).

SECTION 5: STARTING A BUSINESS

IF YOU'RE STARTING A BUSINESS OR WORKING AS AN INDEPENDENT CONTRACTOR, COMPLETE THIS SECTION.

If you are going to start a business, you want to make sure that it makes the best use of your time and natural talents.

Keep in mind, during the first few years of owning a business, you will be doing everything—marketing, sales, accounting, development, administration, and providing the product or service. This means you likely will be using quite a few burnout skills, but it's only temporary.

As your business begins to grow, the goal is to be in a position where you love your day-to-day activities, find your work rewarding, and feel like you are contributing in a meaningful way.

You will find ways to hire people to do the roles and responsibilities you do not want to do and create efficiencies to minimize your time doing them as well.

I always suggest starting a business that already speaks to your Driving Talents and choose work that will activate your Freeing Mindset and meet your needs. For example, if you are in marketing and hate doing social media but love building overall strategy, find a way to do only the strategy.

Maybe you will provide the overall direction while outsourcing the social media work to someone who enjoys it.

If you love managing a business but are not innovative in your business ideas, you might want to explore business franchises.

BRAINSTORM BUSINESSES THAT USE YOUR ON FIRE SKILLS AND DRIVING TALENTS.

Is there an area of expertise or a skill that you enjoy using that you can already monetize? Some examples include software development, marketing, human resources, etc.

1. **List businesses that use your On Fire Skills and Driving Talents:**

_____

_____

_____

BRAINSTORM BUSINESS IDEAS THAT USE YOUR HEATING UP SKILLS (OPTIONAL).

For example, if your Heating Up skill is coaching, perhaps you want to start a life, health, fitness, career, dating, financial, or some other coaching practice.

2. **List business ideas that use your Heating Up Skills (Optional):**

_____

_____

_____

DO YOU HAVE ANY COOL BUSINESS CONCEPTS? (OPTIONAL)

Example:

I'm interested in developing an application X. I don't know how to build apps, but I can figure out how to source the talent.

3. List your cool business concepts (Optional):

_____

_____

_____

ARE THERE ANY BUSINESSES YOU WANT TO EMULATE? (OPTIONAL)

Examples:
- I took my kids to a cool indoor play gym recently. I could see myself following that concept.
- I went to a fashion and makeup consultant five years ago who changed my life; I could see myself doing that type of work.

4. List any business you might want to emulate (Optional):

___

___

___

ARE THERE ANY BUSINESS CONCEPTS THAT YOU THINK YOU COULD IMPROVE UPON? (OPTIONAL)

Example:

I noticed that most career coaches use assessments as a means of getting to know oneself. I want to create a career coaching business that integrates storytelling as well.

5. List any business you think you could improve upon (Optional):

___

___

___

ARE THERE ANY FRANCHISES THAT INTEREST YOU? (OPTIONAL)

Example:

I went to a gym recently and thought, *Wouldn't it be cool if I owned that?*

6. List any franchises that interest you (Optional):

_____

_____

_____

THE LIST

Write down the top four businesses you are interested in researching. Remember, you can always come back and add more to your list, but it is easier to start with four and add more if needed.

7. List the four businesses you want to research.

_____

_____

_____

NEXT STEPS

Now that you have your business list, it's time to dig in and do some research. Skip to Lesson 9: Section 1 (page 170).

LESSON 9

HOW TO DO THE RESEARCH

IF YOU'RE GOING TO CHANGE JOBS, careers, employers, or industries, or start a business, it's important to do your research.

The idea is first to develop an initial understanding of the jobs, careers, employers, industries, or businesses you are considering through online research. You will only get so far researching the internet. It can be hard to pick up the nuances of the different jobs, employers, industries, or businesses out there. Therefore, you will do this preliminary research to make a general assessment about whether the career option would be a good fit. Then, in Lesson 10, you'll move on to career conversations to bring the information you've gathered to life and to start closing in on a better understanding of your options.

> If you are a job or career changer, or starting a business, go to **Section 1: The Job Research Process on page 170.**

> If you are changing employers, go to **Section 2: The Employer Research Process on page 178.**

> If you are changing industries, go to **Section 3: The Industry Research Process on page 182.**

SECTION 1: THE JOB RESEARCH PROCESS

In the last section, you generated a list of jobs or careers to research. In this section, whether you're changing jobs or moving to an entirely different career, you are researching specific job titles within your chosen career. That's why this part of the process is the same for job and career changers - it's about diving deep into specific job titles.

In this process, you will use your True North Guide to evaluate whether the job, career, or business would be a good fit. You will want to assess if the job allows you to use your Driving Talents, aligns with your core values, and uses your On Fire skills. Moreover, does the job pay a salary that fits your needs? Lastly, will the job provide opportunities to grow into other jobs along the career path, if that's something you want?

My two favorite websites to research jobs are:
- the O*Net
- PayScale

Some other websites that clients have had success in doing this stage of research are Glassdoor, Monster, LinkedIn, Idealist, HigherEdJobs, USAJOBS, and Google.

IF YOU ARE LOOKING TO START A BUSINESS:

If you are looking to start a business, complete this section and look at the different jobs you might have in your business. During the startup stage, you will most likely be doing everything from marketing, accounting, sales, and more. As your business grows, you might hire contractors or employees to support you while you're doing more of what you love. If you are going to be a business owner, you have to be realistic and ask yourself if you can tolerate the different jobs you'll have along the way.

Ask yourself, "What job does this business most closely resemble?" Research similar businesses in your area to build a picture for yourself of what your day-to-day might look like. You might need to jump ahead to career conversations with business owners who own similar businesses to understand better what their job looks like on a daily basis.

Please keep in mind, this book does not take you through other aspects of business ownership such as doing your market research, developing a business plan, determining the viability of your business, or the nuts and bolts of running a business. The purpose is to help you identify if the business would create a job that is a good fit for you.

GETTING STARTED:

Now I'm going to walk you through the job research process in depth. Fill in your responses for the first career on your list below. After this, you will repeat the process for the additional careers you wish to research.

If at any time in this process, you realize that a job isn't a good fit, feel free to cross it off your list and move on to the next one without completing all of the questions for that job.

A NOTE ABOUT JOB TITLES:

One of the most frustrating things for job and career changers is figuring out a job title to target. For example, a human resources specialist could also be called a human resources generalist or human resources coordinator, depending on the employer.

One of the reasons you've created your True North Guide is to create a job description for yourself and a guide as to what you want to target.

If you are finding that the O*Net and PayScale do not list the titles you want to research, or you're not sure what job titles to target, then jump to the Career

Conversations section of this book and use your career conversations to help you with your research (page 189).

HOW TO EVALUATE THE SALARY OF THE JOB:

You will want to evaluate the job's salary first. If the job or career path does not pay what you need, as much as you might like the position, that might be a deal-breaker for you, as it is for most people. If the job doesn't pay what you like, cross it off and move to the next one.

The O*Net, PayScale, and Glassdoor include information about the salary of the position. (Remember that here we are talking about a type of position in general terms across various organizations, not a specific job posting for a vacant role.) O*Net aggregates salary information from the Bureau of Labor Statistics. PayScale and Glassdoor analyze anonymous salary data collected from people with similar job titles, years of experience, education, and location. They use an algorithm that gathers information from online job posts.

I often get the question, "How do I decide if I can take a pay cut?" I advise clients to evaluate their finances before making a career change and to discuss the decision with their loved ones. Also, I encourage clients to meet with a financial planner or counselor to discuss their financial situation.

 Be sure to add your salary requirements to your True North Guide (page 20).

 If you find a job that you like, but it doesn't pay what you want, write down the roles and responsibilities or qualities you like about the position in your True North Guide (page 20).

For example, I had a client who explored teaching, but could not afford to live on a teacher's salary. When we met, she asked me about positions that allowed her to teach but would pay more money than a traditional teacher's salary. I told her about training and development, which is a part of human resources, and she ended up pursuing that career instead.

HOW TO EVALUATE THE ROLES AND RESPONSIBILITIES/TASKS:

If you look up a job on O*Net and PayScale, they will have a tasks or roles and responsibilities section. Most job descriptions put the roles and responsibilities that are most important toward the top and least significant toward the bottom.

A lot of companies will use a lot of jargon. If you're unsure what something means, Google it. A little research will give you an idea of the day-to-day. You might also want to explore YouTube videos using search terms such as "a day in the life of X" to learn more about specific jobs.

As you read through that section, ask yourself, "Do I like what I'm reading, and how does it compare to my likes and dislikes, interests, and how I want to spend my time as listed in my True North Guide? If I were to be in this job, do I see myself experiencing my Freeing Mindset or Binding Mindset?" It is important to do a gut check and see how this job feels. What's your gut telling you?

Remember, as you are researching roles and responsibilities, add the ones you haven't done before and that you want to do to your True North Guide (page 20).

WHAT EDUCATION AND QUALIFICATIONS ARE REQUIRED OF THE JOB?

If you're trying to figure out the education and qualifications required for the job, the O*Net has robust resources under the "Job Zone" sections. O*Net will tell you what training and experience are required for the position. You can also click further under the "Credentials" section to research specific certifications or degrees.

When you are doing your research, consider whether you are willing and able to complete the education required for the position. If you are to invest in further education, would it provide the return on your investment both emotionally and financially?

There are many affordable options to pursue further education, such as Coursera, Khan Academy, Udemy, Lynda, edX, Codecademy, Creativelive, and others.

If pursuing a degree is not realistic, certifications might be a better option. I had a client who wanted to become a psychologist but was unwilling to pursue a graduate degree. He decided to explore life coaching programs instead and found a six-month certificate that provided the training they were seeking. I also had a client who liked accounting but did not want to pursue a bachelor's degree. After doing further research, he pursued a bookkeeping certification instead.

As for qualifications for the job or the amount of relevant experience needed, do not assume that if you were to change careers, you would have to start at an entry-level position. Often your previous experience will be relevant to your new role. You just need to find out which positions you should target and how your expertise would transfer to the new type of job. You will learn more when you have career conversations with people who are in the jobs that interest you (page 189).

HOW TO LEARN MORE ABOUT THE INDUSTRY:

If you're trying to learn more about the industry that most employs the job you are researching, O*Net has industry information under the "Wages & Employment Trends" section. You can also Google "key industries that employ [insert job]" to find out which industries employ the job you're researching.

If you want to learn more about the industries, especially if the position is only found in one or a few industries, search for "economic partnership in key industries in [your state]" to learn more.

When you research jobs, it's important to learn about the industry that most often employs that job and to take a look at the industry as a whole. Which values are represented? Do the industry's values align with yours, at least at first glance?

1. Research the rest of the jobs on your list.

Now it's time to research the remaining jobs on your list or different jobs along your career path. Use the chart below to guide you.

JOB TITLE:	
ROLES AND RESPONSIBILITIES LIKES What do I like about the roles and responsibilities of this job?	**ROLES AND RESPONSIBILITIES DISLIKES** What do I dislike about the roles and responsibilities of this job?

THE INNER COMPASS PROCESS

INTERESTS
Does the job align with my interests? Why or why not?

SALARY
What is the typical salary for this job?

Will the salary meet my minimum requirements?

YES/NO

Will the salary range of the career trajectory meet my needs?

YES/NO

EDUCATION REQUIRED
Is my current education sufficient, or am I willing/able to complete the education requirements for this role?

YES/NO

QUALIFICATIONS
How is my background relevant to the position?

CORE VALUES
Would this job meet my core values?

YES/NO/MAYBE

Would the industry of this job meet my core values?

YES/NO/MAYBE

FREEING MINDSET/BINDING MINDSET
If I were to be in this job, do I see myself experiencing my Freeing Mindset or Binding Mindset?

Freeing Mindset / Binding Mindset

DRIVING TALENTS
Does this job allow me to use my Driving Talents?

YES/NO

SKILLS
Will I be utilizing my On Fire and Heating Up Skills at this job?

YES/NO

Will I be avoiding overusing my Burnout Skills at this job?

YES/NO

FINAL VERDICT
Am I still interested in this job?

YES/NO

2. **Based on your online research, list two to three jobs you would like to research through career conversations.**

Look at all the jobs you've researched. Make a list of two to three jobs that excited you. Remember, you can always come back and add more to your list, but it's easier to start with two to three to target your career conversations and add more if needed.

_____

_____

_____

NEXT STEPS

Now that you have your job list, it's time to learn more about the realities of the jobs from the people who are in them. Skip to Lesson 10: Section 1 on page 189. If you're experiencing any doubts or fears about making a career change, skip to page 185.

SECTION 2: RESEARCHING EMPLOYERS

As you research, you're going to use your True North Guide to evaluate whether the potential employer would be a good fit. You will want to assess if the employer pays a salary that fits your needs, is aligned with your core values and interests, and provides opportunities to grow into other jobs along the career path, if that's something you want.

My five favorite websites to research employers:
- PayScale
- Glassdoor
- LinkedIn
- Fortune
- Forbes

Most importantly, it's helpful to go to the organization's website and social media channels to gain some better insights as to what is going on and what is important to them.

HOW TO EVALUATE THE SALARY AND BENEFITS:

The best websites to research salaries by an employer are PayScale and Glassdoor. You might also learn more if you check the employer's employment page because they might list the benefits of working for the employer and offer a salary range listed on the individual job descriptions.

Ask yourself, "What is the salary for the position? What are the benefits listed on the website? Does this employer provide what I need? Remember, you've done a lot of work to identify what's important to you when working for a potential employer during Lesson 4, where you explored your core values. Look on page 18 to see what's important to you.

Also, be sure to add your salary requirements to your True North Guide (page 20).

HOW TO EVALUATE THE MISSION, VISION, AND CORE VALUES OF AN EMPLOYER:

The employer's website will usually share the mission (what they do), vision (the impact they want to make), and core values (their beliefs). If the employer's website does not share this information explicitly, it might be more implicit, such as the services offered and the benefits provided to the customer.

You might learn more through their blog posts and LinkedIn employer page. Notice what the employer shares with its customers and what sort of content they post on social media. What might you infer based on what they share?

Ask yourself, "What do I like and dislike about this employer? Do they align with my interests and core values?"

1. Research the rest of the employers on your list.

Now it's time to research the remaining employers on your list. Use the chart below to guide you.

EMPLOYER:	
EMPLOYER LIKES What do I like about the employer?	**EMPLOYER DISLIKES** What do I dislike about the employer?

INTERESTS
Does the employer align with my interests? Why or why not?

SALARY AND BENEFITS
What is the salary for the position? Does the salary meet my needs?

What are the benefits listed on the website? Do the benefits meet my needs?

CORE VALUES
Would the employer meet my core values?

YES/NO/MAYBE

GROWTH
Does the employer provide opportunities to grow (if that is important to you)?

YES/NO

Is there anything else that is important to me that I want to research about the potential employer?

FINAL VERDICT
Am I still interested in this employer?

YES/NO

2. **Based on your online research, list two to three employers you would like to research through career conversations.**

Look at all the employers you've researched. Make a list of two to three employers that excited you. Remember, you can always come back and add more to your list, but it's easier to start with two to three to target your career conversations and add more if needed.

_____

_____

_____

NEXT STEPS

Now that you have your employer list, it's time to learn more about the realities of the jobs from the people who are in them. Skip to Lesson 10: Section 1 on page 189. If you're experiencing any doubts or fears about making a career change, skip to page 185.

SECTION 3: RESEARCHING INDUSTRIES

As you research, you're going to use your True North Guide to evaluate whether the potential industry would be a good fit. You will want to assess if the industry pays a salary that fits your needs, is aligned with your core values and interests, and provides opportunities to grow into other jobs along the career path, if that's something you want.

My favorite websites to research industries:
- economic partnership and association websites
- the Bureau of Labor Statistics
- O*Net
- PayScale and Glassdoor

Please note, you will most likely end up researching employers that most commonly hire in your industry after you complete the industry research.

HOW TO EVALUATE COMPENSATION:

Identifying compensation by industry can be a little tricky. It takes a bit of reverse engineering. First, identify the industry you want to target, then explore companies within that industry and compensation on PayScale or Glassdoor. Ask yourself, "What is the salary for the position, and will it meet my needs?"

 Be sure to add your salary requirements to your True North Guide (page 20).

HOW TO EVALUATE THE MISSION, VISION, AND CORE VALUES OF AN INDUSTRY:

If you explore economic partnership, association, lobby, and industry websites, you can derive the mission (what they do), vision (the impact they want to make), and core values (their beliefs). You can also learn a lot of industry information by reading the business section of most newspapers and trade magazines.

While mission, vision, and core values can often be employer-specific, you can get a sense of industry trends by doing research.

Ask yourself, "What do I like and dislike about this industry? Does it align with my interests and core values?" Take a look at the industry as a whole. Which values are represented? Do the industry's values align with yours, at least at first glance?

1. Research the rest of the industries on your list.

Now it's time to research the remaining industries on your list. Use the chart below to guide you.

INDUSTRY:	
INDUSTRY LIKES What do I like about the industry?	**INDUSTRY DISLIKES** What do I dislike about the industry?

THE INNER COMPASS PROCESS

INTERESTS
Does the industry align with my interests? Why or why not?

SALARY AND BENEFITS
What jobs are offered in this industry?

What is the salary range of the jobs?

CORE VALUES
Would this industry meet my core values?

YES/NO/MAYBE

GROWTH
Does the industry provide opportunities to grow?

YES/NO

Is there anything else that is important to me that I want to research about the potential industry?

FINAL VERDICT
Am I still interested in this industry?

YES/NO

2. **Based on your online research, list two to three industries you would like to research through career conversations.**

Look at all the industries you've researched. Make a list of two to three industries that excited you. Remember, you can always come back and add more to your list, but it's easier to start with two to three to target your career conversations and add more if needed.

_____

_____

NEXT STEPS

Now that you have your industry list, it's time to learn more about the realities of the jobs from people who are in them. Skip to Lesson 10: Section 1 on page 189. If you're experiencing any doubts or fears about making a career change, skip to page 185.

SECTION 4: OVERCOMING YOUR DOUBTS AND FEARS

If you're experiencing some doubts and fears, please read this section. Of all the parts of the Inner Compass Process, this is where my clients are most likely to lose steam, because the research is where change becomes real. If you're thinking any of these thoughts, know that they're normal. Here are some ideas for shifting out of your bind.

Feeling constricted by the career options →
Go back and widen your options.

Did you limit yourself to jobs that are familiar? Perhaps you are only considering positions that you believe you are qualified for. Instead, broaden your search to find something that draws you in right now. Do not limit yourself.

Karen was a tax attorney and chose to research only legal positions with a different focus, even though they did not excite her. She was frustrated because she didn't like any of her choices. When Karen finally permitted herself to look at jobs outside the law, such as project management and operations, she got excited about the possibilities. Through career conversations, Karen discovered that her skills as a lawyer translated into project management, and she also learned that she did not have to take a step back in her career. Karen eventually made the career change and is a lot happier in her new role.

Frustrated that you haven't nailed down a job title yet →
Trust the process and keep going with career conversations.

Did you find yourself frustrated that you haven't landed a job title that seems right just yet? You might have some titles that you think are just okay or you are just not sure you would like the job. Keep going with this process and jump to Lesson 10 on Career Conversations.

You have written your True North Guide to help you identify the type of job you want, including the roles and responsibilities and how you want to spend your time. A big part of the career conversations is asking people to share titles they think would be a good fit and having them clarify what the day-to-day is like in the position.

Jessica had a digital marketing background and thought she wanted to change careers entirely. She was frustrated because she was excited about organization development but didn't want to go back to school and get a master's degree and struggle with low job prospects.

Jessica shared her True North Guide with a trusted colleague, who suggested she target brand management roles. Jessica initiated several career conversations with brand managers and became excited, because that seemed like a better fit.

You're scared to narrow down your options → Reframe the narrowing down process.

Do you like one or two options but are questioning if that is enough? If you're doing this, reframe your thoughts about narrowing your options as clarifying rather than scary.

Mia found herself attracted to careers in counseling. Other jobs were suggested to her in human resources and higher education, but she just kept coming back to counseling. I told Mia to permit herself just to explore counseling. When she reframed the narrowing process as clarifying, she felt a sense of relief about exploring only the one field that she was interested in.

You're afraid of the unknown → Step into your knowing.

Are you scared that you won't like your new path if you decide to make a change? You've done so much work to get to know yourself throughout this process. Step into your knowledge and own it. Commit to making changes that are in alignment with your knowledge. They don't have to be big changes, such as changing careers entirely; they can be small, such as changing jobs within your employer.

Doug was a junior rabbi at his synagogue. While he loved his congregation, he knew he would never be promoted to senior rabbi and make the impact he wanted to make through his work. He wanted a congregation that promoted social justice, but the safety of his current role was compelling.

Doug had to step into his knowing that he wanted to work with a congregation that valued social justice and was active in making an impact on their local community. Doug ended up moving to a different state and taking a position as a senior rabbi at a synagogue. He felt so rewarded by stepping into his knowing and doing the work that was calling him.

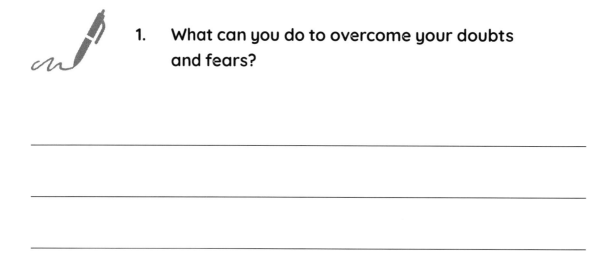

1. What can you do to overcome your doubts and fears?

LESSON 10

CAREER CONVERSATIONS

NOW THAT YOU'VE NARROWED DOWN your career options, it's time to test the waters. The best way to learn about a job, career, employer, or business is through career conversations—talking to people doing work that interests you. You'll learn the realities of the positions, career fields, employers, or industries so that you can make informed choices about a career.

WHAT IS A CAREER CONVERSATION?

A career conversation is a meeting between a person who wants to learn about a career (you) and someone who is currently in the career (interviewee). It lasts for fifteen to thirty minutes and can be over the phone, on an online meeting platform, or in person.

You're not there to ask for a job but to tap someone's expertise and get information about the career that interests you.

WHY HAVE CAREER CONVERSATIONS?

Career conversations (more commonly known as informational interviews) are essential for finding the right career fit for you. The more people you meet and the more time you research the careers you're interested in, the more you will intuitively know whether they align with your true north.

Meet your mentors.

Think about the most famous stories in books and movies. The heroes almost always benefit from the support of mentors and teachers. Career conversations can help you find your mentors and teachers, the people who provide support and guidance as you continue your journey.

Looking back on your childhood, schooling or earlier times in your career, can you think of any mentors who guided you along the way? That could be a teacher who inspired you, a friend who helped you widen your social circle, or a therapist who helped you better understand yourself. Take a minute to reflect on the ways that person changed your life.

As you have career conversations, you may meet one mentor, or you may meet many people who offer you a little boost.

Find your tribe.

As we meet people in specific careers, industries, companies, and more, we may connect interpersonally with some more than others.

I had a client who was choosing between a marketing career and a career as a therapist. Even though she thought she was better suited for marketing, she found that she connected with therapists much more easily. She was initially disappointed that she didn't connect with people in the career she thought she wanted. I helped her realize that this was valuable information about which career would suit her better.

The way we feel around other people gives us information about whether the career could be a good fit. Even if you're on the more introverted side, there might be a sense of ease when you speak to people who are in a career that might be just right. These conversations can help you find your tribe. The positive feelings you have when you're with your tribe are a good indicator that the career might be a good fit for you.

Narrow down your job options.

Through your career research, you've probably narrowed down the types of jobs you want to target. Career conversations help you reduce your list even further and feel more confident in your decision. It's a way to test the waters before investing any more time or money into making a change.

Gain confidence.

Career conversations will help you feel more confident when you have job interviews. You'll also gain insider information, industry knowledge, and jargon about the careers you are interested in.

Tap the hidden job market.

In addition, you'll be able to tap the hidden job market. Statistics show that 75 percent of jobs aren't even advertised on popular websites such as Indeed or LinkedIn. When you start to meet people who are in the field you're interested in, you're going to learn about opportunities that may not be advertised online.

Build trust.

Career conversations are also opportunities to build trust with individuals and companies that can hire you. Hiring preferences are often given to candidates that are known to the employer. HR professionals have shown me scorecards showing that points are awarded to candidates who already have shared familiarity with the employer.

Assuage your fears.

You will also have the chance to ask questions about the things you fear. It's scary to make a career change, and career conversations help you understand the realities of a career. You will read more about fears further on.

USE YOUR CAREER CONVERSATIONS AS YOUR GPS

 Throughout this process, I want you to keep coming back to your intuition. Pay attention to how you feel when you talk to people. After a conversation, do you feel light and expansive in your body? Or do you feel tightness or contraction? Your physical and intuitive sensations are there to guide you toward a good career fit.

HOW TO HAVE CAREER CONVERSATIONS: OVERVIEW

Career conversations consist of three main parts:

- preparation
- the conversation itself
- the follow-up

In the next sections, I'll be diving deep into each of these and showing you how to set yourself up for the most successful career conversations possible.

Preparing for your career conversations

First, you will make a list of candidates to contact. Then you'll email them, and, finally, you'll prepare for the conversations.

You should come out with a list of three to five people (the more, the better) to approach for career conversations.

Brainstorm and think of everyone you know. Look at your Facebook and LinkedIn networks, your phone contacts, and anything else that will help you gather a list of contacts.

You can identify people you want to talk to and then work backward to find connections, or you can speak to the people you know and see if they know anyone that works in a career you're researching. Either way works fine.

For example, you may want to connect with someone who works at a particular employer. Do you have any friends or acquaintances that have connections to that employer? Reach out and see if there is anyone with whom they can connect you.

Or you might know that your friend Sue knows a lot of people. Ask her if she knows anyone in the job, career, employer, industry, or business you want to research. If she does, ask if she'll send an email introduction.

If you don't have any direct connections to a particular job, career, employer, industry, or business, it can help to connect with trade associations, alumni networks, and professional associations.

 1. Brainstorm: Who do you want to ask for a career conversation?

Fill in three to five names and email addresses below. Write your intention behind reaching out. Perhaps that person might tell you about a job or career path, or maybe they can share insights regarding their employer or industry.

NAME	EMAIL ADDRESS	INTENTION

REACH OUT NOW.

Do not lose momentum or put this off until tomorrow. Reach out to the person right now and ask them to have a conversation with you. You can use this template to reach out to them, or you can check out these informational interview templates from the website DiversityJobs: https://www.diversityjobs.com/2019/02/informational-interview-e-mail-templates/

Dear (Insert Name),

I found your name through [x] and am interested in speaking with you about your [career/organization/position/industry/business/educational background].

I have a background in [x], and I'm working for [x] doing [x].

My main goal is to gather more information about [x] because I'm considering [pivoting/changing] my career and would love your insight. Could I ask for twenty minutes of your time over the phone, Zoom, coffee, or lunch? My treat!

Would you be available during the following?

x

x

Please let me know if one of those dates and times works for you, where you would like to meet, or a good number to reach you, and I'll send over a calendar invite. I appreciate your time, and I look forward to hearing from you!

Sincerely,

Your Name

Email Address

Phone Number

I recommend reaching out to more than one person at a time, as you never know how long it will take someone to get back to you.

When they do respond, put the meeting on your calendar immediately. Respond by thanking them and letting them know you're looking forward to the conversation.

If you're feeling nervous about reaching out

Keep in mind that most people want to help and support others. I know that when I've been asked for career conversations, I was happy to offer my support. When I started my business, many people helped me along the way. I'm pleased to be of service to others and give back. I think generosity has a way of coming full circle.

Also, people typically like talking about their jobs and their experiences, so they will likely enjoy the conversation as much as you do.

If you're shy, you can even do a career conversation with a family member or friend for practice.

PREPARE FOR THE CONVERSATION.

If someone agrees to have a career conversation with you, research that person's background and educational history, just as you would do for a job interview. You want to do this for two reasons. First, you want to make a good impression. Second, it will help you think of questions explicitly about them. Also, research the job and career itself so you can go into the conversation well informed.

 2. Before your meeting, research your interviewee and their employer. What is their position, what is their educational background, and what is their career history?

You can use Google, Facebook, LinkedIn, their employer website, and any other resource.

PERSON'S NAME	
JOB POSITION	
EDUCATIONAL BACKGROUND	
CAREER HISTORY	

3. List four to eight questions you would like to ask your interviewee. (Refer to the list of questions on page 204 for ideas.)

_____

_____

_____

4. Who is the one person you want to connect with after you meet with your interviewee (e.g., name, position, duties, etc.)?

DURING YOUR CAREER CONVERSATIONS

Be generous.

Your interviewee is giving you their time and attention. If you are meeting the interviewee in person, repay their kindness by buying them a drink if you're at a coffee shop, or by bringing coffee to their office. If you are meeting your interviewee at their office, ask what type of drink they want beforehand so you can get something they like.

If you are a mid-to-late-career professional and your interviewee is an executive, perhaps you might want to take them for a nice meal. Consider your audience and treat them accordingly.

If you speak to the person over the phone or Zoom, a thoughtful thank-you email is sufficient for repaying their kindness.

Start your interview with a thank you.

Greet your interviewee and thank them for their time. Make sure they know you appreciate their meeting with you.

Ask your four to eight questions.

Ask the questions you prepared. Take notes on their answers, but don't worry about capturing every word they say. It's more important to make a personal connection and get the gist of what they tell you.

Let it flow naturally.

If other questions come up, go with it. This is a conversation, so let it develop naturally.

End the conversation with an offer and an ask.

At the end of the conversation, thank your interviewee for their time. Ask them, "Is there anything I can do for you?" The person you are interviewing may not have anything they want from you, but you never know. You ask this as a way of showing your appreciation and generosity.

I once had a college student ask an interviewee, "Is there anything I can do for you?" and their interviewee responded that they were struggling with their smartphone. My client's impromptu tutoring session made such an impression that it helped them land a job interview.

Additionally, end your conversation by asking your interviewee if they have one contact they can introduce you to—and be specific (name or job title). The more specific you are, the easier it will be for your interviewee to think of who they can introduce you to. If your interviewee has someone in mind to introduce you to, request an email introduction to that person (you can even follow up with an email template to make the introduction). If the interviewee does not have time to make an introduction, ask them if they would be comfortable with you using them as a reference.

Exchange business cards.

If you meet the interviewee in person, obtain your interviewee's business card and give them one of yours at the end of the conversation. You can say something like, "Before we leave, do you have a business card so I can follow up with you?" If you or your interviewee are not carrying a business card, that's okay. Just make sure you have their contact information so that you can follow up!

FOLLOW UP AFTER YOUR CAREER CONVERSATIONS.

Send a thank-you note immediately.

Remember to follow up by sending a thank-you note, either via email or regular mail. Put some thought into the thank-you note. Mention something you appreciated from your conversation or something you learned from your interviewee.

A strong thank-you note can make a huge difference in helping you stand out. An interviewee will be more inclined to support you if they feel appreciated.

Keep in touch.

Follow-up is just as important as the conversation itself because it's where you can build some of your most important relationships. As I shared previously, career conversations can lead to mentorship, networking opportunities, friendships, job leads, and more!

Do not get into the mindset that you are developing these relationships to get a job. I encourage the mindset of building professional relationships to nurture your career—similar to building relationships to support you in other areas of your life. This will support you in being authentic and remaining open to all outcomes.

Here are some ideas of how you can nurture your professional relationships. If most of your follow-up is focused on giving or connecting rather than getting something, your interviewee should be happy to receive it.

- Send an email after you talk to a person they connected you to.

- If you read an article that pertains to your conversation, forward it and let them know it made you think of them.
- Send birthday and holiday cards or emails.
- Ask them for advice.
- Introduce them to other people in your network.

Ask for job connections.

Once you've built a rapport with the interviewee, you may want to ask them to connect you to people who are hiring. You can ask:

- I noticed a posting for X job. Will you please introduce me to the hiring manager?
- Would you be comfortable passing my résumé on to the hiring manager?
- Do you know of any positions that will be opening soon?
- What's the best way for me to get my foot in the door with . . . ?
- If I wanted to obtain a job here, what would be the best way to learn of job vacancies?

MY EXPERIENCE WITH CAREER CONVERSATIONS.

About ten years ago, I searched for a job because I wasn't enjoying my position as a case manager. I found case management wasn't aligned with my talents and skills, and I knew I wanted to change to do more outreach to youth. I asked all of my friends if they had any connections with nonprofits who worked with youth, and I was introduced to Brian, who was the director of a school-based nonprofit organization. I asked Brian if he would be willing to meet with me for twenty minutes over coffee. Our conversation ended up lasting an hour because we had so much to talk about.

At the end of the meeting, Brian was comfortable passing my information on to other nonprofits in the area that worked with youth. I met with several nonprofits. After every career conversation, I circled back to Brian to let him know how the meeting went and to thank him for the introduction.

About a month and a half after meeting Brian, I noticed a job posting on the company's website for a position in youth outreach. I emailed him and asked if he would be comfortable passing my résumé along to the hiring manager. About a week after that email, I was called in for a job interview, and two weeks after that, I was offered a position.

> Career conversations can lead to job opportunities, as long as you stay in touch with the people you meet.

THE EVOLUTION OF CAREER CONVERSATIONS.

The process of career conversations will change a bit as you have more of them. In the beginning, you will just be gaining information about the job. But as you continue, your understanding will deepen, and you will gain clarity. You will be drawn toward some careers and away from others.

In the beginning, you'll be asking general questions such as:
- What do you like/dislike about your job?
- What does a typical day look like in this role?
- What is a typical career path in this field or organization?
- What percentage of your time is spent doing each function?
- What is the most important thing that someone planning to transition into this career should know?

If you feel that you haven't landed the right job title, as your career conversations evolve, it often helps to share your True North Guide with your interviewer and allow them to guide you toward related job titles that might be a better fit. You might share something along the lines of, "I've done X in the past, but I'm looking for something that allows me to do X in the future. What titles would you suggest I target?" You might even ask for introductions to people who have the job titles that the person suggests you target.

As you become more familiar with the career, employer, industry, or business, your questions will become more specific.
- In what ways is your occupation changing?
- Is this industry heavily regulated?
- What constraints, such as time and funding, make your job more difficult?
- Do you foresee the opening of new markets? Do you predict the development of new products/services?
- What technologies does the employer use for X?
- What obstacles do you see getting in the way of the employer's profitability or growth?

I also suggest that you ask questions to help you identify whether the career aligns with your values. I also encourage you to ask questions to help you alleviate your fears.

Below are two charts. One chart offers questions based on values. The other chart provides examples of questions based on fears.

Take some time to highlight the questions below, and you can use them in your career conversations to help you decide if a career is a good fit for you.

THE INNER COMPASS PROCESS

YOUR VALUE	QUESTIONS TO ASK (QUESTIONS IN THE WHITE ARE CAREER-SPECIFIC; THE ONES IN GRAY ARE EMPLOYER-SPECIFIC.)
AUTONOMY AND FREEDOM	• How much flexibility do you have in determining how you perform your job? • Is your work primarily individual or group-oriented?
	• What's the hierarchy like at this organization? • Is there flexibility in work hours, vacation, remote work, place of residence, etc.?
PASSION	• What are your interests, and in what way does this job satisfy your interests? • Are there aspects of your job that are repetitive? • What projects have you worked on that have been particularly interesting? • What particular skills or talents are most essential to be effective in your job? • If you could do things all over again, would you choose the same path for yourself? • My interests are X. Do you have any suggestions of job titles that might be more appropriate for me?
	• What do you like most about this employer? • Would you describe your company culture as passionate?
STABILITY	• In what ways is your occupation changing? • How is the economy affecting this industry? • What trends do you think will affect someone entering the field right now? • How much job security do you have in this line of work? • What kinds of work do you feel prepared to do with your background? • Is there a salary ceiling?
	• How does your employer differ from its competitors? • How optimistic are you about the employer's future?
GROWTH AND LEARNING	• What does growth look like in this field? • How rapidly do people move to the next level in this career? • What type of trainings would you suggest I take to enter this field? • Which professional journals and publications should I be reading to learn about this career?
	• What does growth look like with this employer? • Does your employer offer professional development? • What kind of training programs does your employer offer? • Is there tuition reimbursement?

ACHIEVEMENT	• What does it take to be successful in this field/industry? • What were the keys to your career advancement? • How competitive is this field? • How does a person progress in your field? • What are the highest-level positions one can hold in this career? • How rapidly do people move to the next level in this career?
	• What does it take to be successful in this company? • What does it take to get promoted in this company? • Is the management style more top-down? • How competitive are you with your coworkers? • How does the employer evaluate your job performance? • How does the employer reward its employees? • What are the advancement opportunities within this employer?
WORK/LIFE BALANCE	• What type of sacrifices have you had to make to be successful in this career? Were they worth it? • What hours do you usually work? • Do you have to put in much overtime or work on weekends? • Do you take work home with you? • Are there other obligations outside work hours? • How has your job affected your lifestyle? • What creates the most amount of stress in your job?
	• Is there flexibility in work hours, vacation, remote work, place of residence, etc.? • What type of benefits does your employer offer? • Does your employer offer family and medical leave? • What hours do you usually work? • Do you have to put in much overtime or work on weekends? • Do you take work home with you?
CONNECTION	• What is your relationship like with your customers/clients? • What is your relationship like with your supervisor/coworkers?
	• What systems are in place to provide feedback? • What is your relationship like with your supervisor/coworkers? • Do people socialize together outside of work? • Can you tell me more about the culture? • Is the management style more top-down? • What resources and support does your employer offer?
PEACE/EASE	• Do you have to deal with a lot of conflict in your role? • What kind of problems do you deal with daily? • What are the major frustrations of this job? • What creates the most amount of stress in your job?
	• Is there a great deal of turnover at this employer? • How would you describe the morale of your coworkers? • Can you tell me more about the culture?
CREATIVITY	• What does creativity look like in this career? • Are there certain positions/roles that are more creative than others?
	• What does the employer do to foster innovation and creativity?

THE INNER COMPASS PROCESS

YOUR FEAR	QUESTIONS TO ASK
DO I NEED TO GO BACK TO SCHOOL? OR AM I PURSUING THE RIGHT EDUCATIONAL PATH?	• What would be the best kind of training to transition from my current career to your career? • What types of certifications, credentials, or licenses are required? • Is graduate school recommended? • How well did your educational experience prepare you for this job? • What courses or certifications have proved to be the most valuable to you in your work? • What courses do you wish you had taken that would have prepared you? • What do you feel is the best educational preparation for this career?
HATING MY JOB.	• I enjoy doing X. What type of position would you suggest I target? • The things I like the most about my current career are X. Will I find some of those same things if I switch to your career? • The things I dislike the most about my current career are X. Will I encounter any of those same challenges in your career?
TAKING A STEP BACK.	• What position would you suggest I target? • What's the best way for me to get more experience in your field without taking major steps backward from the level to which I've progressed in my current career? • What sacrifices do you think I might have to make the switch into your career field? • Do you know of other professions where I would have to take a step back?
WILL SOMEONE HIRE ME?	• My current career is X. How easy or difficult do you think it might be to make a transition? • The skills I use the most in my current career are X. To what extent and in what ways do you think those skills are transferable to your career? • What aspects of my background do you feel would be the biggest hurdle for me in making a transition? • What skills do you think I need to develop? • Do you know of anyone who has made a similar transition? How did it work out? • If I am unable to obtain a position in this field, what other fields would you recommend?
HOW WILL I FIND A JOB?	• What organizations/associations would you suggest I join? • How did you get your job? • What jobs and experiences have led you to your present position? • What is the typical job-interview process like for this type of position? • Could you take a brief look at my résumé and make suggestions? (*Note: I suggest you ask this question to someone you have a strong rapport with, or if a person asks to see your résumé.) • What is the best way to obtain a position that will get me started in this career? • What type of experience, paid or unpaid, would you suggest for anybody pursuing a career in this field? • What should I do to prepare myself for emerging trends and changes in this field? • How would you assess the experience I've had so far in terms of entering this field? • What qualifications would you be looking for if you were hiring for a position such as yours?

OTHER WAYS OF TESTING THE WATERS:

In addition to career conversations, there are several ways to test the waters.

For job seekers:
- job shadowing
- volunteering
- taking free online courses

If you're a job seeker, a great way to see the day-to-day realities of a job is to shadow someone in that job. You can also volunteer at the organization to see it from an insider's perspective. If there are any skills you will need to learn for the job, take free online courses to get an in-depth view of what you need to learn.

For potential students:
- auditing classes
- reaching out to professors
- reading course catalogs

If you're considering going back to school to get credentials for a new position, see if you can audit classes. Reach out to professors for career conversations. Peruse course catalogs to understand better what types of courses you would be taking.

For business owners:
- shadowing a business owner in a similar field
- having career conversations with business owners
- taking online classes

If you want to start a business, you can shadow or talk to a business owner in a similar business to your own. Be careful, though, because some business owners may see you as the competition and may be reluctant to help you out. You can also take online classes to learn more about what it takes to be a business owner in your field.

5. What additional methods would you like to use to test the waters?

MY PLAN	HOW I'M GOING TO IMPLEMENT IT
Job shadowing	Contact X and ask if I can shadow him at work.

PART 3

CREATING A MAP OF NEXT STEPS

LESSON 11

NARROWING YOUR OPTIONS

THE PROCESS OF TESTING THE WATERS has given you a lot of new information about the careers in which you're interested. Unlike when you initially evaluated the careers, you now have tangible, personal experience related to those careers, whether that's career conversations, job shadowing, taking courses, or other forms of testing the waters.

You can now evaluate your career choices with greater clarity than before. First, you're going to check in with your intuition to see whether your job, career, employer, industry, or business choices feels right to you. Then you're going to check back with your True North Guide to see if they are still a good fit.

CHECK IN WITH YOUR INTUITION.

Take a minute to check in with your intuition. Based on everything you've just written, does this career still feel like a good fit? There are many different ways your intuition may communicate with you. I have shared four of the most common ways in the chart below. You may want to check in with one or more of these.

Ways your intuition communicates with you:

PHYSICALLY	You may feel a tightening of your chest, an expansive feeling in your belly, shortness of breath, or heaviness in your limbs. There are many ways your intuition communicates physically. One way to determine how your body communicates is by thinking "No" and seeing which sensations arise, and then thinking "Yes" and seeing which sensations arise then. You can then connect these to your physical sensations around the career you're evaluating.
VERBALLY	You may hear the words in your mind, either a resounding "Yes!" or a deadening "No!"
VISUALLY	You may see images of yourself in a career that are either negative or positive.
GUT FEELINGS	You may just have a feeling of rightness or wrongness about the career.

1. **Take a minute and connect with your intuition. Does this job, career, employer, industry, or business feel like a good fit? Why or why not? Write whatever comes up.**

_____

_____

_____

CHECK BACK WITH YOUR TRUE NORTH GUIDE.

When you first began doing career research, you asked some important questions about whether each career was a good fit, according to your True North Guide. Now that you've completed some career conversations, and checked in with your intuition, it's time to circle back and re-evaluate the careers.

Please check with your True North Guide and fill in the charts below according to what you've now learned about your job, career, employer, industry, or business.

TWO QUESTIONS HAVE BEEN ADDED TO THESE CHARTS:

What does my intuition say about this job, career, employer, industry, or business?

You checked in with your intuition in the last section, so you can copy and paste your answer below.

Do I feel like I've met my tribe?

Now that you've completed some career conversations, you probably have a better sense of whether the people in this job, career, employer, industry, or business are a good fit for you. Write down a few words about what you've discovered.

| If you are a job, career change, or starting a business, go to **Section 1, page 214.** | If you are exploring a change of employers, go to **Section 2, page 215.** | If you are exploring changing industries, go to **Section 3, page 217.** |

SECTION 1: EXPLORING A JOB CHANGE, CAREER CHANGE, OR STARTING A BUSINESS:

JOB TITLE:	
ROLES AND RESPONSIBILITIES LIKES What do I like about the roles and responsibilities of this job?	**ROLES AND RESPONSIBILITIES DISLIKES** What do I dislike about the roles and responsibilities of this job?
INTERESTS Does the job align with my interests? Why or why not?	
SALARY What is the typical salary for this job? Will the salary meet my minimum requirements? YES/NO Will the salary range of the career trajectory meet my needs? YES/NO	**EDUCATION REQUIRED** Is my current education sufficient, or am I willing/able to complete the education requirements for this role? YES/NO
CORE VALUES Would this job meet my core values? YES/NO/MAYBE Would the industry of this job meet my core values? YES/NO/MAYBE	**FREEING MINDSET/BINDING MINDSET** If I were to be in this job, do I see myself experiencing my Freeing Mindset or Binding Mindset? Freeing Mindset/Binding Mindset

DRIVING TALENTS Does this job allow me to use my Driving Talents? YES/NO	
WHAT DOES MY INTUITION SAY ABOUT THIS JOB?	**DO I FEEL LIKE I'VE MET MY TRIBE?**
SKILLS Will I be utilizing my On Fire and Heating Up Skills at this job? YES/NO Will I be avoiding overusing my Burnout Skills at this job? YES/NO	**FINAL VERDICT** Am I still interested in this job? YES/NO

SECTION 2: EXPLORING A CHANGE OF EMPLOYERS:

EMPLOYER:	
EMPLOYER LIKES What do I like about the employer?	**EMPLOYER DISLIKES** What do I dislike about the employer?

THE INNER COMPASS PROCESS

INTERESTS
Does the employer align with my interests? Why or why not?

SALARY AND BENEFITS
What is the salary for the position? Does the salary meet my needs?

What are the benefits listed on the website? Do the benefits meet my needs?

CORE VALUES
Would the employer meet my core values?

YES/NO/MAYBE

WHAT DOES MY INTUITION SAY ABOUT THIS EMPLOYER?

DO I FEEL LIKE I'VE MET MY TRIBE?

GROWTH
Does the employer provide opportunities to grow (if that is important to you)?

YES/NO

IS THERE ANYTHING ELSE THAT IS IMPORTANT TO ME THAT I WANT TO RESEARCH ABOUT THE POTENTIAL EMPLOYER?

FINAL VERDICT
Am I still interested in this employer?

YES/NO

SECTION 3: EXPLORING AN INDUSTRY CHANGE:

INDUSTRY:	
INDUSTRY LIKES What do I like about the industry?	**INDUSTRY DISLIKES** What do I dislike about the industry?

INTERESTS
Does the industry align with my interests? Why or why not?

SALARY AND BENEFITS
What jobs are offered in this industry?

What is the salary range of the jobs?

CORE VALUES
Would this industry meet my core values?

YES/NO/MAYBE

WHAT DOES MY INTUITION SAY ABOUT THIS INDUSTRY?

DO I FEEL LIKE I'VE MET MY TRIBE?

GROWTH Does the industry provide opportunities to grow? YES/NO	
IS THERE ANYTHING ELSE THAT IS IMPORTANT TO ME THAT I WANT TO RESEARCH ABOUT THE POTENTIAL INDUSTRY?	
FINAL VERDICT Am I still interested in this industry? YES/NO	

SECTION 4: STRUGGLING TO NARROW DOWN YOUR CAREER OPTIONS?

If you're struggling to narrow down your career options, read this section for some strategies to help you move forward.

Why you're struggling: Nothing is exciting you.

Solution: Have more career conversations and test the waters.

When clients are often not excited about their options, it is often because they haven't had enough career conversations or they haven't addressed their fears in their career conversations. Keep in mind, some clients need to speak to five to ten people before they land on the job, career, employer, industry, or business they want to switch to.

If you're not getting excited about any of your options after career conversations, go back and talk to the people whose job, career, employer, industry, or business interested you the most and ask for a follow-up conversation. The purpose of your follow-up conversation is to ask more questions to address your fears and to ask for more introductions to other people in the field.

When you speak to your interviewee, share something along the lines of, "I liked X about this career, but didn't like X. Are there other options (job titles, employers, or industries) you would recommend?" After the interviewee has offered their suggestions, ask if they know of anyone they can introduce you to who could share more advice and information.

For example, Greg was most interested in a social work career but was unsure if it was the right fit based on the two career conversations he had with social workers. He was completely turned off by case management, and he feared that clinical counseling could potentially lead to burnout.

I asked Greg if he felt comfortable reaching out to someone with whom he had already had a career conversation to ask some follow-up questions. Greg felt comfortable reaching back out to his sister's best friend.

Greg was able to share his concerns with her and ask for more introductions to other social workers. After having four more career conversations, Greg learned that there are many career options besides case management and clinical counseling, such as policy, community outreach, and programmatic positions if he took the appropriate graduate school classes.

Greg decided to test the waters by sitting in on some graduate school classes and job shadowing a few of the social workers he met through his career conversations. Greg decided to pursue his Master of Social Work after gaining more clarity about the various job options he would have upon graduating.

> **Why you're struggling: You're afraid of the unknown.**
>
> **Solution: Turn the unknown into the known.**

Are you scared that you won't like your new path if you decide to make a change? Right now, your "new path" is a hazy idea in your mind. That's why it feels scary. But as soon as you start doing career conversations, job shadowing, and job interviews, your options will become more tangible. When you put yourself out there, you will begin meeting people and learning about jobs, and you will get excited about some of the opportunities.

Most of my clients don't know if they will like a position until they are in the job interview. They either get a really good feeling or not. Then, if they are offered the position, they can make a decision based on their intuitive sense about it.

Even in the unlikely event that you accept a position, try it, and don't like it, you can still change. I've had clients who left their jobs within the first three months because they didn't like their employers or pivoted again because they found that they didn't like their new jobs.

The beauty of your True North Guide is that it will help you identify what isn't working more quickly so that you can make a shift. You don't have to be worried about being "stuck" in a job that you don't like, because you have all the tools you need to find something more aligned.

William, a forty-seven-year-old physical therapist, decided to go into sales after completing the Inner Compass Process. The first three months at his new job were terrific. He loved his work, liked his supervisor, and thought he had made the right move. Then his supervisor was fired. His new boss micromanaged him and was unsupportive and critical. We tried different attempts to see if he could have a good working relationship with his boss, but it just wasn't a good fit. William also went to HR to see if he could switch to another department and found that he had no other options within the company.

Luckily, because of his career conversations, William had a healthy network. He reconnected with people he had spoken to previously and one of them helped him get another sales job. The position was a better fit, and he ended up staying at his company for four years.

1. What can you do to narrow down your options?

_____

_____

_____

WHERE IS YOUR INNER COMPASS GUIDING YOU NEXT?

Now that you've checked in with your intuition, permit yourself to move forward with the option that seems like the best move for now. Trust yourself. Remember, you can always change your mind or go back to what you've been doing. You have learned so much information about yourself that whatever change you make will be more aligned because you've done the deep work.

What job, career, industry, employer, or business do you want to pursue? Remember, you can target your search to multiple options and see which one pans out.

2. **What change(s) do you want to pursue? Add it to your True North Guide (page 20).**

_____

_____

_____

LESSON 12

MAKE A POST-IT TIMELINE

YOUR POST-IT TIMELINE IS:
- your goals
- the strategies to help you achieve your goals
- tactics to overcome the obstacles that might get in your way

Now it's time to make your plan for your next steps—whether you change your job, career, employer, industry, or start a business.

When I've worked with job changers, they often think they need to plan their next steps in complete detail. Instead, a better use of time is to understand high-impact job search strategies and put together a flexible plan.

Your Post-It Note Timeline contains your goals, strategies to achieve your goals, and tactics that you will use to overcome obstacles that get in your way.

A Post-It Timeline idea is that it is a working document that is nimble and can shift as you discover what works and let go of what doesn't work.

When you plan, keep in mind that some things will inevitably be out of your control—a meeting will be canceled or postponed, a strategy you try will not work, or you might be rejected after a job interview.

On the other hand, there will be strategies you attempt that might go well and that you find are a better use of your time—networking with a particular group yields better results, you find a mentor, or you might be offered a job after an interview.

You will want to change your timeline to adjust to the strategies that work.

GOALS, STRATEGIES, AND TACTICS

Let's break down the difference between a goal, strategy, and tactic.

A goal is a benchmark you would like to achieve, and the strategy is the action you take to get there. Some examples of goals are to obtain a job, land an interview, or start a business. Examples of strategies are to fill out résumés, schedule career conversations, work with a recruiter, or hire a business coach.

There are two types of obstacles that get in people's way of achieving their goals: external and Binding Mindsets. Some examples of external obstacles are children, a poor economy, and a busy schedule. **As defined by this book, a tactic is an action you take to help you overcome any obstacle you might encounter**. There are two types of obstacles that get in people's way of achieving their goals: external obstacles and Binding Mindsets. Some examples of external obstacles are taking care of children, a poor economy, and a busy schedule. To overcome external obstacles, you might use tactics such as arranging childcare, networking to tap the hidden job market, or carving out time in your schedule for your job search. In this process, you will likely experience your Binding Mindset as well. For example, if you experience a lack of motivation or confidence, tactics that might be helpful include reaching out to others, practicing self-empathy, and working with a job search coach.

Here's the kicker. Your goals have to feel completely aligned with your True North Guide, but the strategies you use to accomplish your goals might push you slightly out of your comfort zone. For example, you might be clear you want a raise, and being paid more money for your work feels right, but the strategy of talking to your supervisor and negotiating a pay increase might be slightly uncomfortable.

Throughout these next few sections, you will be working to identify your goals, strategies, and tactics so that you have clear next steps and a timeline to get there.

HOW TO APPROACH YOUR POST-IT NOTE TIMELINE:
- First, I will help you set your one to two goals and your timeline.
- Then, we'll reverse engineer and explore the strategies to help you achieve your goals.
- After, we'll look at the obstacles that might get in your way from achieving your goals and then develop tactics to overcome those obstacles.
- Finally, we'll mark your calendar, so that you are set to go.

MATERIALS NEEDED FOR YOUR POST-IT NOTE TIMELINE:
- Post-Its of different colors and sizes
- a large piece of paper or cardboard with a line drawn on it
- pens and markers of different colors and sizes

I know that many people do their planning on the computer. However, when you use physical paper and sticky notes, it helps you move your body and your energy. It's amazing how much more easily your ideas flow when you are connected to your body.

Before we get started, draw a line across your paper. Select specific colors to represent your goals, your strategies, and your tactics. Be creative! Have fun with this and enjoy the process.

SETTING GOALS

Grab the stack of Post-Its you've designated for your goals. As you write down your goals, you will copy them on to your Post-Its.

In this section, you will come up with goals and your timeline to achieve them. **Your goals are the major benchmarks you want to accomplish,** and the timeline of achieving your goals is totally up to you, whether you choose a year, six months, or three months from now.

Your goals might include changing your job, career, employer, industry, or starting a business. You could also set goals such as writing a book, adjusting your schedule for more free time, taking a vacation, or anything else that is important to you.

For each goal, ask yourself:
- Is it realistic?
- Does it feel right intuitively?

Set realistic goals.

When you bring your goals into the "real world" and begin executing them, they must be realistic, because otherwise, it is easy to get derailed. Your goals should feel both exciting and doable.

It might also help to research how long it has taken others to achieve similar goals so that you are mentally set up for success.

Check in with your intuition.

Check your intuition about your goals and take a minute to listen to any messages that come up. They might be words you hear, visuals you see, a feeling in the pit of your stomach, or just a gut feeling of rightness or wrongness. Be sure to listen to your intuition when it comes to your goals because when you do, you're more likely to follow through.

WHAT IS YOUR BIG-PICTURE GOAL THAT YOU WANT TO ACHIEVE? WHAT IS YOUR TIMELINE?

Are you working in a new job or career, or launching a business that's aligned with your True North Guide? Maybe you've scheduled more days off, a vacation, and free time into your schedule? Go to page 222 to review your next move.

1. What is your big-picture goal?

_____

_____

_____

2. What is your timeline for achieving this goal?

One year, six months, three months?

_____

_____

_____

Write down your goal on a Post-It and place it at the end of your timeline. For example, you might write "Find a new job, six months."

WHAT IS YOUR GOAL(S) AT THE MIDPOINT OF YOUR TIMELINE? WHAT IS YOUR TIMELINE?

Now let's tackle the goal(s) that is at the midpoint of your timeline.

Some goals at the midpoint of your timeline can include finding a mentor, growing your network to five close contacts, narrowing down the companies you want to target, navigating the final round of job interviews, or submitting your résumé and cover letter to X number of employers.

If you're looking to start a business, maybe you have the initial draft of your business plan, built a business website, or hired someone to support you with your marketing strategy.

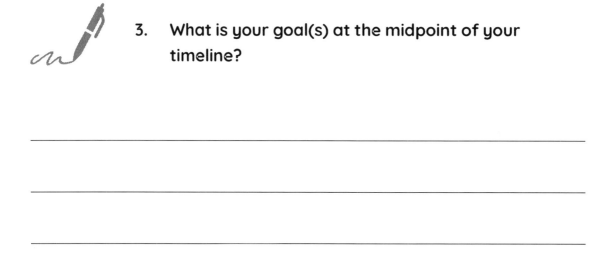

3. What is your goal(s) at the midpoint of your timeline?

___

___

___

4. What is your timeline for achieving this goal?

One year, six months, three months?

_____

_____

_____

Write down your goal on another Post-It and place it in the middle of your timeline. For example, you might write, "Interview at three different companies, three months."

5. Where are you today? What have you already accomplished?

Take a minute to write down what you've already accomplished. You may already be part way to your goals. Be proud of all you've done already. Completing this book is a great accomplishment within itself.

_____

_____

_____

Write down your current accomplishments on another Post-It and place it at the beginning of your timeline. For example, you might write, "Did four career conversations and am targeting a new job."

SETTING STRATEGIES

Now pick up the stack of Post-Its you've chosen for strategies. You will be writing them down and placing them on your Post-It timeline.

This is the part you've been waiting for—the section where you create an actionable plan for achieving your goals! **Strategies are the actions you take to get to your goals.**

I've created a menu of action steps you can use, such as updating your résumé, preparing for a job interview, and others. Some of them are one-time activities, while others are things you may do again and again. Before you dive in, here are some guidelines for choosing strategies that will work for you.

*Note: If you are looking to start a business, I would reach out to your local Small Business Development Center to receive support with strategies to help you launch your business.

Pick strategies that will help you stay in your Freeing Mindset.

When you are in your Freeing Mindset, you have more energy, feel better, and can accomplish more. Use what you know about yourself to choose strategies that will help you stay in your Freeing Mindset and away from your Binding Mindset.

For example, if you're an introvert, you may not want to go to networking meetings or large industry events, but you may feel comfortable setting up career conversations where you can talk one-on-one and have deeper conversations.

Push yourself outside your comfort zone.

Remember, choose some strategies that might push you out of your comfort zone, but not to the point where you shut down. For example, if you are an introvert, setting up career conversations may be slightly uncomfortable for you, but you do it because they have a high impact.

Choose higher-impact strategies, if you can.

For each strategy, I've rated it by the amount of impact it will have. For example, sending your résumé and cover letter into an online job posting is lower impact than having a career conversation.

If you feel comfortable with higher-impact strategies, I suggest you try them out. They will hopefully help you get a job in less time than the lower-impact ones.

Know that your strategies may change over time.

Remember, this plan is a living document. Your strategies will likely change over time as you see what works and what doesn't.

If you don't know how to implement all your strategies . . .

There is an abundance of high-quality free tools online and in-person: https://ncda.org/aws/NCDA/pt/sp/resources

https://www.careeronestop.org/LocalHelp/WorkforceDevelopment/workforce-development.aspx

Be realistic.

Just as you set realistic goals, make sure you are realistic in choosing your strategies, as well. Set yourself up for success by taking an honest look at your time and energy and then adopting strategies that you can implement.

Use the chart below to select strategies for your plan.

TYPE OF STRATEGY	IMPORTANCE	IMPACT	FREQUENCY
UPDATE YOUR PROFILES			
Update your résumé. You can use resources such as your local workforce center, your alumni career services, a website such as Novorésumé, or hire someone to assist you.	High	Medium	Ongoing
Update your cover letter. You can use resources such as your local workforce center, your alumni career services, or hire someone to assist you.	Medium	Low	Ongoing
Update your LinkedIn. You can use resources such as your local workforce center, your alumni career services, or hire someone to assist you.	High	High	One time
Update your social media (Facebook, Twitter, etc.) with your professional background.	Low	Low	One time
Update your portfolio and personal website if needed.	Medium	It Depends	One time
Set up accounts and sign up for job boards.	Low	Low	One time
INTERVIEWING			
Practice interviewing.	High	High	Ongoing
Prepare/practice your elevator pitch.	High	High	One time
Prepare and practice negotiation.	High	High	One time
NETWORKING			
Career conversations	High	High	Ongoing
Employer prospecting	Medium	Medium	Ongoing
Associations	High	High	Ongoing
Alumni network	Medium	Medium	Ongoing
Job search support groups (Meetup.com)	High	High	Ongoing
Career fairs	Medium	Medium	One time
Recruiters	Low	Medium	One time

Cold calling or emailing	Medium	High	Ongoing
TRAINING AND GETTING JOB EXPERIENCE			
Volunteering	High	High	Ongoing
Internships	High	High	Ongoing
Job shadowing	High	High	One Time
Classes/trainings	Medium	Medium	Ongoing

6. **What strategies would you like to use to help you get to the midpoint of your timeline?**

Write them down below, along with the timeline in which you would like to accomplish them.

STRATEGIES	TIMELINE

Write down your strategies on different Post-Its and place them in order of when you'll do them from now to the midpoint of your timeline. For example, you might write "Complete your new resume by week 2" or "Hire a resume writer by week 2."

7. Choose the strategies you would like to use from the midpoint to the end of your timeline.

Write them down below, along with the timeline in which you would like to accomplish them.

Note: You can fill in strategies now if you want, or you can leave this blank and come back to fill it in three months from now when you have a clearer sense of where you need to go from here.

STRATEGIES	TIMELINE

Write down your strategies on different Post-Its and place them in order of when you'll do them from the midpoint to the end of your timeline. For example, you might write "Research salary negotiating by week 10" or "Practice interviewing by week 12."

TACTICS TO OVERCOME OBSTACLES

Congratulations on setting goals and strategies! Before we move on, let's make sure there isn't anything coming up in your life that would keep you from meeting them.

What obstacles might get in your way of achieving your goals? Are they more internal, such as lack of motivation or confidence, or are they more external, such as family obligations, the demands of your current job, or a weak economy?

No matter what, obstacles will come up. The trick is to be ready for them and have some tactics to help you overcome them. **A tactic is an action you take to help you overcome your obstacles.**

Now grab the stack of Post-Its that you have chosen for tactics. You will be writing your tactics and adding them to your timeline.

WHAT EXTERNAL FACTORS MIGHT GET IN THE WAY OF YOU MEETING YOUR GOALS?

Are there any known outside factors that may keep you from meeting your goals and strategies?

These may include:
- moving (whether within the same city or across the country)
- having kids
- taking care of a relative
- your partner changing jobs
- planning for a big event, such as a wedding

If you have something planned that will affect your goals, please write it onto your timeline. This could include trips, weddings, moving, and other life cycle events.

8. What tactics can you use to overcome these obstacles?

These may include:
- reading some articles online
- talking to people who have been through a similar situation
- asking for advice
- working with a coach

_____

_____

_____

Write down your tactics on different Post-Its. For example, you might write "Work with a coach" or "Ask for advice."

Some of my clients choose to put their tactics along one of the borders of the timeline. Others put them where they'll think they'll need them in the process.

For example, you may be limited on time between your current job and your family. You might ask your partner to watch the kids for four hours a week so that you can focus on your job search. You may place that Post-It on your timeline as the first step you take, within the next day or two.

Or you may know that you have a big trip coming up in two months. You might organize your calendar to be intentional about how you spend your time and what you're going to do to account for being away. You may place this Post-It before and during your trip on your timeline.

HOW MIGHT YOUR BINDING MINDSET GET IN THE WAY OF YOUR GOALS?

Now let's look at how your Binding Mindset may get in the way of you meeting your goals. Do you withdraw, self-criticize, tell yourself that a change is not realistic, or lose motivation?

9. What tactics can you use to overcome your Binding Mindset?

The good news is that you've done a lot of work already to identify them and support yourself during Lesson 3 on countering your Binding Mindset (page 67). Add how you plan to counter your Binding Mindset here.

_____

_____

_____

Write down your tactics on different Post-Its. For example, you might write "Work with a coach" or "Meditate in the mornings." You can choose to use a new color of Post-Its or change your marker color to differentiate these from your other tactics.

My clients will often place tactics to overcome their Binding Mindsets along the borders of their timelines or wherever feels intuitive.

PUT YOUR PLAN ON YOUR CALENDAR.

Take a look at your Post-It Note Timeline. You should be proud! You've worked hard to clarify your next steps.

Now, we want to make sure you follow through, and the best way to do this is to put it on your calendar. I want you to take a few minutes now to put your plan on your calendar to ensure that you implement it. Whether you use Google Calendar or a paper planner, pull it out and add the relevant parts of your timeline.

The more you make your career change a routine, and block off times on your calendar to prioritize it, the better. I find it helpful to block one or two hours a day to work on my goals and have it as a part of my daily routine.

NOTE FROM THE AUTHOR

I'M SO EXCITED YOU MADE IT to the end of this book! I'm so proud of you. While this was a simple process, it was not easy.

You started this journey by digging deep, going back to your childhood, and looking at key memories that influenced who you are today. You discovered your Freeing and Binding Mindsets, your core values, and your Driving Talents. Then you transitioned into identifying the best use of your time and skills, what you want to step into, and what you want to let go of. After that, you researched the changes you want to make to meet your needs better—changing jobs, careers, employers, industries, or starting a business. Lastly, you made a timeline of the next steps to accomplish your goals.

You had to dig deep; you had to go outside your comfort zone. Whether you decide to make a smaller shift in your current work or a more considerable shift such as changing careers, your hard work will pay off because more of your needs will be met.

If I could have you take anything away from this book, it's for you to know that your needs are important. The more aware you are of your needs and the more you make it a priority to meet them, the more fulfilled you will be. Bringing awareness to your needs and prioritizing them is one of the highest forms of self-love. When you love and care for yourself, you have more capacity to love and care for others.

Do not be afraid to listen to your inner compass and allow it to lead you to your new career. As you've learned, your feelings, thoughts, and behaviors are a doorway to understanding your needs. When you have a moment of uncertainty or have a gut feeling that something is off, spend some time with it. Get to know it. Ask it questions. There's so much wisdom within you—all you need to do is tap it. When in doubt, go back to the wisdom of your True North Guide.

Unless you are close to retirement, my guess is this next job will not be your last one. As you journey through your career, you might end up taking positions that highlight different uses of your time and skills and adjust for your changing needs, so your career will need to adapt. However, your Freeing Mindset, Binding Mindset, core values, and Driving Talents will not change. Whenever you are ready for the next evolution of your career, the Inner Compass Process will be here to support and guide you to your next steps.

When in doubt, ask for help. Seek the support of mentors, teachers, therapists, and loved ones.

I know you can do it. You are important, you are worthy, and you are loved—just for being you.

With love,
Danielle

NEEDS INVENTORY

PHYSICAL WELL-BEING
air, food, movement/exercise, rest/sleep, safety, shelter, touch

SAFETY
security, stability, support

CONNECTION
affection, belonging, cooperation, communication, closeness, community, companionship, compassion, consideration, consistency, empathy, inclusion, intimacy, love, mutuality, nurturing, respect/self-respect, to know and be known, to see and be seen, to understand and be understood, trust, warmth

ESTEEM
acceptance, appreciation, respect/self-respect

HONESTY
authenticity, integrity, presence

PLAY
joy, humor

PEACE

beauty, communion, ease, equality, harmony, inspiration, order

AUTONOMY

choice, freedom, independence, space, spontaneity

MEANING

awareness, celebration of life, challenge, clarity, competence, consciousness, contribution, creativity, discovery, efficacy, effectiveness, growth, hope, learning, participation, purpose, self-expression, spirituality, stimulation, to matter, understanding

(Needs Inventory (c) 2005 by Center for Nonviolent Communication
Website: www.cnvc.org Email: cnvc@cnvc.org
Phone: +1.505.244.4041)

LIST OF FEELINGS WHEN YOUR NEEDS ARE SATISFIED

AFFECTIONATE
compassionate, friendly, loving, open-hearted, sympathetic, tender, warm

ENGAGED
absorbed, alert, curious, engrossed, enchanted, entranced, fascinated, interested, intrigued, involved, spellbound, stimulated

HOPEFUL
expectant, encouraged, optimistic

CONFIDENT
empowered, open, proud, safe, secure

EXCITED
amazed, animated, ardent, aroused, astonished, dazzled, eager, energetic, enthusiastic, giddy, invigorated, lively, passionate, surprised, vibrant

GRATEFUL
appreciative, moved, thankful, touched

INSPIRED
amazed, awed, wonder

JOYFUL
amused, delighted, glad, happy, jubilant, pleased, tickled

EXHILARATED
blissful, ecstatic, elated, enthralled, exuberant, radiant, thrilled

PEACEFUL
Calm, clear-headed, comfortable, centered, content, fulfilled, mellow, quiet, relaxed, relieved, satisfied, serene, still, tranquil, trusting

REFRESHED
enlivened, rejuvenated, renewed, rested, restored, revived

(Feelings Inventory (c) 2005 by Center for Nonviolent Communication Website: www.cnvc.org Email: cnvc@cnvc.org. Phone: +1.505.244.4041)

POSITIVE BEHAVIORS LIST

active	gregarious
ambitious	kind
amiable	logical
caring	organized
charismatic	persuasive
compassionate	pleasant
confident	polite
conscientious	precise
considerate	quiet
creative	reflective
curious	self-assured
engaged	self-aware
enthusiastic	sensitive
faithful	sincere
friendly	talkative

(List of Words that Describe Behavior
Website: https://grammar.yourdictionary.com/word-lists/list-of-words-that-describe-behavior.html)

LIST OF FEELINGS WHEN YOUR NEEDS ARE NOT SATISFIED

AFRAID
apprehensive, dread, foreboding, frightened, mistrustful, panicked, petrified, scared, suspicious, terrified, wary, worried

ANNOYED
aggravated, dismayed, disgruntled, displeased, exasperated, frustrated, impatient, irritated, irked

ANGRY
enraged, furious, incensed, indignant, irate, livid, outraged, resentful

AVERSION
animosity, appalled, contempt, disgusted, dislike, hate, horrified, hostile, repulsed

CONFUSED
Ambivalent, baffled, bewildered, dazed, hesitant, lost, mystified, perplexed, puzzled, torn

DISCONNECTED
alienated, aloof, apathetic, bored, cold, detached, distant, distracted, indifferent, numb, removed, uninterested, withdrawn

DISQUIET
agitated, alarmed, discombobulated, disconcerted, disturbed, perturbed, rattled, restless, shocked, startled, surprised, troubled, turbulent, turmoil, uncomfortable, uneasy, unnerved, unsettled, upset

EMBARRASSED
ashamed, flustered, guilty, mortified, self-conscious

FATIGUE
beat, burnt out, depleted, exhausted, lethargic, listless, sleepy, tired, weary, worn out

PAIN
Agony, anguished, bereaved, devastated, grief, heartbroken, hurt, lonely, miserable, regretful, remorseful

SAD
Depressed, dejected, despair, disappointed, discouraged, disheartened, forlorn, gloomy, heavy-hearted, hopeless, melancholy, unhappy, wretched

TENSE
anxious, cranky, distressed, distraught, edgy, fidgety, frazzled, irritable, jittery, nervous, overwhelmed, restless, stressed out

VULNERABLE
Fragile, guarded, helpless, insecure, leery, reserved, sensitive, shaky

YEARNING
Envious, jealous, longing, nostalgic, pining, wistful

(Feelings Inventory (c) 2005 by Center for Nonviolent Communication
Website: www.cnvc.org Email: cnvc@cnvc.org. Phone: +1.505.244.4041)

LIST OF NEGATIVE BEHAVIORS

aggressive
anxious
argumentative
avoidant
bossy
careless
clingy
closed-off
controlling
deceitful
distracted
domineering
flaky
guarded

impatient
inconsiderate
judgmental
loner
manipulative
reserved
rigid
rude
scatterbrained
serious, spiteful
undisciplined
volatile
withdrawn

(List of Words that Describe Behavior
Website: https://grammar.yourdictionary.com/word-lists/list-of-words-that-describe-behavior.html)

LIST OF DRIVING TALENTS

advising
calculating
cheerleading
clarifying
creating
coaching
communicating
connecting
contributing
designing
directing
expressing
guiding
harmonizing
humor
ideating
implementing
including
inventing
inspiring
intuiting
judging

leading
listening
loving
logic
logistics
mediating
mentoring
negotiating
networking
peacemaking
perceiving
persuading
planning
puzzle-solving
teaching
strategizing
storytelling
understanding
visioning

ABOUT THE AUTHOR

DANIELLE MENDITCH ROESSLE is a licensed clinical social worker in the state of Colorado and global career development facilitator/instructor with the National Career Development Association. She earned her Bachelor of Social Work from Arizona State University and her Master of Social Work from the University of Denver.

As the founder of Inner Compass Coach, she uses a unique blend of career development and psychology to help her clients get unstuck and guide them toward a fulfilling and financially rewarding career.

Danielle has presented her one-of-a-kind approach for career transition in articles in the National Career Development Association's *Career Convergence* magazine, SkillScan, SharpHeels, the *Glendale Cherry Creek Chronicle*, and the *Coloradoan*.

ACKNOWLEDGMENTS

MANY PEOPLE HAVE INFLUENCED the Inner Compass Process and have supported the writing of this book.

A special thank you to Robert Wood of Spirit Aura, Nora A'Bell of Revenue Tribe, and the work of Dr. Marshall Rosenberg, founder of Nonviolent Communication, as they have influenced the rediscovery portion of this book.

I took a workshop with Robert Wood of Spirit Aura back in 2013, and he showed me how our obstacles of overcoming lead to life purpose. I'm so grateful for that experience because it started the foundation of the Inner Compass Process.

I also got to work one-on-one with Nora A'Bell back in 2014 when she was building her employer, Revenue Tribe. Nora influenced my concepts and interconnections of the Freeing Mindset, Binding Mindset, core values, and Driving Talents. Her work is brilliant, and I encourage everyone to explore her programs.

The piece that wove everything together was when I read Marshall Rosenberg's *Nonviolent Communication* (NVC) back in 2016. I finally understood that our needs drive everything we do, which form our core values. I was able to deepen my knowledge of NVC while training with Kathy Ziola MA, CNVC Certified Trainer and owner of Communication Works.

The career exploration part of my program has been influenced by the Facilitating Career Development curriculum of the National Career Development Association. I want to thank Linda Sollars of Creating Purpose, who informed my knowledge of career exploration because she trained me as a career development facilitator back in 2014.

A special recognition goes to Christiana Kelman, LCSW, and Stacey MacGlashan,

LCSW, who peer-reviewed the Inner Compass Process as I was creating it. They helped me understand the psychology around inner-child work and how to weave it into career counseling.

I also want to acknowledge Chuck Blakeman of Crankset Group, who helped me build my business. Chuck would preach that we should maximize the best use of time and talents to help our businesses thrive, which I now apply to my clients in assisting them to flourish in their careers.

Daniela Uslan and Michelle Tullier, this book could not have been written without you. I'm grateful for your help with writing this fantastic book and for help translating this process to make it accessible to others.

Andrew Goldman of Your In House Law, Kathleen Ammalee Rogers of Positive Vision Network, my husband, Ian Roessle, and my family, Bruce, Debbie, and Jackie, thank you for being my cheerleaders.

And lastly, I want to give a big shout-out to my clients. I appreciate your feedback and support as I honed this process throughout the years. I couldn't have done any of this without you.

REFERENCES

1. Yogman, M., Garner, A., Hutchinson, J., Hirsh-Pasek, K., & Golinkoff, R. M. (2018). The Power of Play: A Pediatric Role in Enhancing Development in Young Children, https://pediatrics.aappublications.org/content/142/3/e20182058, Date accessed: January 8, 2021

2. Freudenrich, C., & Boyd, R. (n.d.). "How Your Brain Works", HowStuffWorks.com, https://science.howstuffworks.com/life/inside-the-mind/human-brain/brain.htm, Date accessed: January 8, 2021

3. Byron, K. (2021). The Work of Byron Katie, https://thework.com/, Date accessed: January 11, 2021

4. Stillman, C. (2016). Self Sabotage with 3 Malas, https://vimeo.com/187241898/418dd1adb1, Date accessed: January 8, 2021

5. The Inner Compass skills assessment was inspired by the SkillScan test developed by Lesah Beckhusen, https://www.skillscan.com/about/author, Date accessed: January 11, 2021

6. Pope, L. (2009). 6 Tips for Navigating Your Human Resources Career Path, https://learn.g2.com/human-resources-career-path, Date accessed: December 30, 2020

Made in the USA
Middletown, DE
04 May 2021